THE CURIOUS CAT

AND THE QUEST FOR SCHOOL IMPROVEMENT

THE CURIOUS CAT

AND THE QUEST FOR SCHOOL IMPROVEMENT

DR WAYNE CRAIG

amba press

For my grandchildren –
Zach, Liam, Harvey, Sophie, and Mackenzie –
whose questions, wonder, and laughter inspire this book
more than they know.

You remind me every day why curiosity matters.
May you grow to be literate, numerate – and endlessly curious.
May you ask questions that open doors,
pursue learning that lifts others,
and carry a sense of wonder all through your lives.

This book is for you – and for the questions still to come.
Just be sure to save a few for me.

Published in 2025 by Amba Press, Melbourne, Australia

www.ambapress.com.au

© Wayne Craig 2025

All rights reserved. No part of this book may be reproduced or transmitted in any form or by any means, electronic or mechanical, including photocopying, recording or by any information storage and retrieval system, without prior permission in writing from the publisher.

Cover design: Tess McCabe
Internal design: Midlands
Editor: Andrew Campbell

ISBN: 9781923403246 (pbk)
ISBN: 9781923403253 (ebk)

A catalogue record for this book is available from the National Library of Australia.

Contents

About the Author		vii
Acknowledgments		ix
How to Read This Book: Terms and Tools That Matter		xi
Prologue	The Return of the Curious Cat	1
Chapter 1	A Known Unknown – Why Curiosity Matters	3
Chapter 2	School Improvement Has Stalled	25
Chapter 3	Moral Purpose and the Rhythm of Reform	38
Chapter 4	School Capital – The Conditions for Growth	53
Chapter 5	Reawakening Inquiry – Practices That Bring Curiosity to Life	71
Interlude	Before the Shadow Falls	79
Chapter 6	The School Improvement Tree – Growth from the Inside Out	81
Chapter 7	Through the Socioeconomic Shadow – Curiosity and Equity	108
Chapter 8	Leading for Inquiry, Equity, and Change	124
Chapter 9	Unleashing the Curious System – Scaling Inquiry with Integrity	138
Chapter 10	The Cat's Next Step – Sustaining a Movement Over Time	157
Epilogue	In the Company of Questions	174
Appendix A	Research Summary and Methodology	175
Appendix B	Implementation Guides	179
Appendix C	Self-Reflection Tools	189
Appendix D	Self-Assessment Tools	203
Appendix E	Literary and Cultural Touchstones	212
References		215

About the Author

Wayne Craig is an Australian teacher, school leader, curriculum consultant, and researcher whose work has been shaped by a consistent belief: that every child deserves to leave school literate, numerate, and curious. This simple idea has remained constant through decades of change – as a classroom teacher, principal, system leader, and now doctoral researcher.

For Wayne, literacy and numeracy have never been narrow goals. They mean more than decoding text or performing calculations. They involve the ability to absorb, retain, and apply knowledge – to make sense of information, to solve problems, and to act thoughtfully in a changing world. Coupled with curiosity, they form the foundation for a meaningful education. That combination has shaped his approach to pedagogy, leadership, and system reform.

In his early years as a teacher, Wayne was closely involved in school-based reforms that brought rigour and flexibility to student learning. He worked to open up personalised learning pathways, ensuring all students had access to challenge and choice.

As a principal, he led a school that set high expectations but moved away from unnecessary constraints. There were no bells or uniforms, but there was structure, trust, and a belief in student voice. Respect, responsibility, and engagement were non-negotiable. He supported vocational education, embraced emerging technologies, and built partnerships with organisations like the AFL and Tennis Victoria to expand what was possible.

Later, as a regional director, Wayne led improvement efforts across more than 200 schools and early learning centres. He co-founded Powerful Learning with Professor David Hopkins and helped establish the Koorie Academy of Excellence with the Victorian Aboriginal Education Association – both grounded in equity, cultural inclusion, and student agency.

He brought the same focus to his work with McREL International, co-authoring widely used tools and resources on curiosity, learning, and leadership that have influenced professional learning in Australia and internationally.

Throughout, Wayne kept returning to one question: *Why do some schools succeed in creating and sustaining deep improvement while others struggle?* That inquiry became the basis of his doctoral research, examining the interaction of school socioeconomic status, workplace curiosity, moral purpose, and school capital in shaping student outcomes. This book shares what he found – offering practical insights for educators, leaders, and system actors working to build more just, curious, and effective schools.

Now working as a writer and consultant, Wayne stays close to the work of schools and systems. He continues to learn alongside educators, grounded in the belief that lasting change grows from inside communities – not from compliance, but from shared purpose, trust, and thoughtful inquiry.

When not working with schools, Wayne spends time with his family and friends – still reading, still asking questions, still walking the path of learning.

The Cat, it seems, still walks beside him.

Acknowledgments

This book is about people. The ideas in these pages – curiosity, moral purpose, shared leadership – didn't come from theory or policy. They came from schools. From teachers and principals, students, and families. From hard days, quiet wins, mistakes, and trying again.

Three people who have had a lasting impact on how I think and lead are David Hopkins, John Munro, and Ramon Lewis. I've worked closely with all three and am proud to call them friends. Each, in different ways, has helped me sharpen my focus, deepen my thinking, and stay anchored in what matters. More than anything, they've reminded me – by example – that leadership is about care, trust, and the will to keep learning. Curiosity and improvement aren't extras. They are the work.

I've also worked with teachers, principals, and support staff who carry this work every day. They are too many to name – and I hesitate to list names for fear of leaving someone out – but I do want to mention Tina, Bill, Wilma, Lochie, Costa, Kristele, Fernando, Jo, Deb, Eleanor, Liz, Anesti, Catherine, Jim, Peter, Heather, Pat, Maureen, Marilyn, Lynne, Lyn, Geoff, Glenn, and David. Each of you has made a mark – on your schools, on your students, and on me.

At the system level, I've had the chance to work with people who stayed steady through tough times. Angela, Graham, Peter, Vic, Anna, Rob, Claude, Susan, David, Joe, Celestine, Ron, Jim – and the admin teams who kept the show running – thank you. I've learnt a lot from your judgment, your timing, and your patience.

Working with Tim Waters, Bryan Goodwin and the McREL team in Denver was a turning point. Our work on the *Curiosity and Powerful Learning* series stretched my thinking and opened new doors. It remains one of the most rewarding professional experiences I've had.

I also want to thank three close friends – Bob, Robin, and John. You've been there in the background, steady and supportive, never needing to be asked. Sometimes it was a quiet word; other times just knowing you were there. It mattered.

To Professor David Gurr and Associate Professor Lawrie Drysdale – thank you for your wise counsel, encouragement, and steady belief both in the work and in me. Your generosity, insight, and good humour made the doctoral journey not only possible but genuinely rewarding. I'm deeply grateful.

And to my family – Sandra, Lucas, Mitchell, and Emily – you've lived through all of it. The early mornings, the late nights, the stretches where I was elsewhere in body or in mind. You've brought honesty, humour, perspective, and care. You've kept me grounded, even when I lost my way. Tennielle and Bethany – thank you for your kindness and perspective. You're part of this too.

If the book says anything worth hearing, I hope it's this: real school improvement starts with people – with purpose, with questions, and with the courage to keep going.

To those carrying the work forward – quietly, bravely, without waiting for permission – the Cat will be watching.

How to Read This Book: Terms and Tools That Matter

Before we begin, a note on language. This is a book about schools, systems, and the people who shape them – and like any big conversation, it has its own vocabulary. Some terms in these pages are familiar but used in particular ways; others are introduced as metaphors or frameworks to bring complex ideas to life. What follows is not a dictionary but a guide: a way to travel with clarity through the ideas ahead. You don't need to memorise them – maybe keep them close, like a compass in your pocket. As the journey unfolds, you may find new meanings emerge. That's part of the work. That's part of the wonder.

A guide to the core terms and metaphors used in this book

The language we use shapes how we think and act. This guide captures some of the core terms and metaphors used throughout the book, offering a shared vocabulary for schools, leaders, and systems seeking to foster curiosity, purpose, and collective improvement.

Term	What it means
Adaptive expertise	A professional capacity to inquire into one's impact and adapt practice in response – combining deep knowledge with continual learning.
Culture of inquiry	A school environment where questions drive improvement and learning is everyone's shared responsibility.

Term	What it means
Curious leadership	An approach to leadership that fosters inquiry, asks good questions, models reflection, and builds collective learning.
Curiosity	A mindset of wonder, questioning, and active exploration – about students, teaching, and systems.
Good work	Teaching that is excellent in quality, personally meaningful, and socially responsible – aligned with personal values and collective purpose.
Inquiry	A disciplined way of asking, listening, reflecting, and adapting to improve practice and outcomes.
Inquiry compass	A leadership guide with four essential directions: listening, learning, leading with questions, and navigating complexity.
Inquiry stance	A way of approaching daily professional work – teaching, leadership, and system design – with curiosity, reflection, and a commitment to continual learning.
Moral purpose	A deep commitment to doing what is right for students, especially those most often left behind.
School capital	The collective resources a school draws upon to improve: intellectual, social, organisational, and financial capital.
School improvement tree	A visual metaphor showing how improvement grows from moral purpose (roots), through school capital (trunk), to curiosity and strong outcomes (canopy).
The Curious Cat	A metaphor for curiosity itself: curious, watchful, irreverent, and unafraid to ask difficult questions. The Cat represents inquiry as a quiet but persistent force – ready to return where it is welcomed. Not a mascot, but a spirit that nudges, listens, and helps schools stay alive to possibility.

The journey at a glance

This book is structured around three essential questions, simple in form but powerful in implication. These questions shape the chapters ahead and offer a pathway through complexity.

Where are we now?

We begin by examining the state of schools today – how curiosity has been marginalised, how reform has become mechanical, and how purpose and capital are too often undervalued.

Chapters 1-4:

- Chapter 1: A Known Unknown – Why Curiosity Matters
- Chapter 2: School Improvement Has Stalled
- Chapter 3: Moral Purpose and the Rhythm of Reform
- Chapter 4: School Capital – The Conditions for Growth

Where are we headed?

We explore a more human future – where learning is inquiry-rich, equity-focused, and morally grounded. These chapters imagine what happens when curiosity takes root again.

Chapters 5-7:

- Chapter 5: Reawakening Inquiry – Practices That Bring Curiosity to Life
- Chapter 6: The School Improvement Tree – Growth from the Inside Out
- Chapter 7: Through the Socioeconomic Shadow – Curiosity and Equity

How do we get there?

We move from imagination to implementation – focusing on leadership, systems, and scaling curiosity with integrity.

Chapters 8-10:

- Chapter 8: Leading for Inquiry, Equity, and Change
- Chapter 9: Unleashing the Curious System – Scaling Inquiry with Integrity
- Chapter 10: The Cat's Next Step – Sustaining a Movement Over Time

Whether you're an educator, a leader, or a system thinker, this map is here not to constrain your reading but to guide it. You may choose to travel sequentially or to enter where your questions are loudest.

The Cat doesn't mind where you begin. Only that you begin – curiously.

Prologue: The Return of the Curious Cat

*'We're all mad here.' – The Cheshire Cat,
Alice's Adventures in Wonderland*

There was a time when curiosity was woven through the life of a school. You could see it in the bright, bold questions of students. You could hear it in the hum of teachers puzzling together over practice. You could feel it in leaders who made time for learning – not as an extra but as the heart of the work.

These moments weren't exceptional. They were part of the daily rhythm of schooling. They reminded us that education is, at its best, an act of shared inquiry.

But over time, that rhythm changed. Systems grew tighter. The pace quickened. The work became measured and monitored. Teachers became implementers. Students became performers. And curiosity – that fragile, essential thread – was pushed to the edges of the fabric. Not lost, but often overlooked.

The Cat noticed.

In this book, the Curious Cat is a metaphor – a gentle guide for what has always lived in good education: the instinct to wonder, to notice, to ask. The Cat is not a program, nor a policy. It is the spirit of inquiry itself. It slips through cracks in the system. It curls beneath the edges of performance data. It waits in the questions we haven't yet asked.

And when we choose to notice again, it is ready to return.

This book is about making room for that return – about seeing curiosity not as a soft extra but as a central force that can renew teacher agency, deepen student learning, and bring life back to the system itself. The journey here is not one of silver bullets or quick fixes. It is about cultures, relationships, and purposes that help curiosity take root – and stay.

You will encounter three enduring ideas:

- **Curiosity** as a spark for learning and growth
- **Moral purpose** as the ethical root of educational practice
- **School capital** as the enabling conditions through which curiosity can thrive.

Through it all, the Cat will walk with us – not loudly, not in charge, but present. A reminder that even in the most structured system, there is space for questions. There is space for learning. And there is always a way back.

The door is open.

The Cat has noticed.

Let's begin.

CHAPTER 1
A Known Unknown – Why Curiosity Matters

BIG IDEAS IN THIS CHAPTER

Curiosity is foundational, not frivolous. It is a deep human drive essential for learning, innovation, and growth – yet rarely prioritised in education reform.

Despite global calls for creativity and inquiry, education systems often suppress curiosity through standardisation, performative compliance, and risk aversion.

Curiosity is a 'known unknown' – widely acknowledged but seldom cultivated systemically. It slips through the cracks of policy and practice.

To reclaim curiosity, we must challenge narrow definitions of success, reframe uncertainty as a resource, and invite wonder back into the centre of school life.

This chapter asks:

- What happens when curiosity disappears from schools?
- What does it take to bring it back – and let it thrive?

'Curiouser and curiouser!' – Lewis Carroll

When curiosity faded

There was a time when curiosity felt more present in the daily life of many schools – not everywhere, not always, but often enough to leave a trace. You could hear it in classroom conversations that spiralled into deeper questions rather than arriving at tidy conclusions. You could see it in the way teachers gathered to share hunches and puzzles, not just plans and programs. Leadership, in some settings, meant making space for thoughtfulness as much as delivering direction. Inquiry was not yet a strategy – it was a habit, woven into practice through shared questions, emerging ideas, and professional trust.

This kind of culture didn't come with a label or a framework. Strategic plans did not codify it, nor did system directives mandate it. But it was real. It lived in the professional discretion of teachers, the collegial debates over practice, the willingness of leaders to say, 'I don't know – let's find out.' Curiosity was part of the air that schools breathed. This approach shaped how problems were tackled, relationships were built, and progress was achieved – not uniformly, but through reflection, dialogue, and iteration.

But over time, this habit eroded. Policy narrowed. Testing expanded. Accountability metrics tightened. The system, once loosely held together by professional trust and moral purpose, became more rigid, more risk-averse, more focused on what could be measured rather than what mattered. Teachers became implementers. Students became performers. And curiosity, while never extinguished, receded to the edges. It showed up as a side project, an enrichment task, or an optional professional learning day. But it stopped being central. It became what Donald Rumsfeld famously called a 'known unknown' – something everyone sensed was missing but struggled to name, much less restore (Rumsfeld, 2002).

What makes this erosion particularly troubling is its subtlety. It didn't arrive with warning bells or dramatic upheaval. Instead, it crept in quietly, policy by policy, decision by decision – so gradually that many didn't notice until the habits of inquiry had already faded. This slow drift gave the illusion of continuity, even as the underlying culture changed. And because the new norms – performance metrics, league tables, mandated strategies – were framed as neutral or inevitable, their impact on professional judgment and learner agency often went unquestioned. The real loss, then, wasn't just curiosity itself but the conditions that had once allowed it to flourish. By the time many schools recognised what had shifted, the space for questions, experimentation, and wonder had already been carved out and replaced with compliance.

The metrics that began to dominate public education policy – NAPLAN scores, ATAR results, standardised growth charts – were designed to improve equity and raise performance. And sometimes, they offered useful insights. But the hardening of these measures into the primary lens for judging success narrowed the space for genuine exploration. When schools are under pressure to improve results quickly, the safest course is often to double down on what's already known – more explicit instruction, more tightly sequenced content, more drilling of key skills. Innovation becomes a risk. Curiosity becomes a luxury. The unintended consequence is that some of the very qualities schools claim to nurture – critical thinking, creativity, resilience – are crowded out by a system that values certainty over insight.

Of course, not all schools succumbed to this trend. There have always been educators who protected curiosity in their classrooms, often quietly and without recognition. They are the ones who turned curriculum into questions, who carved out time for reflection even when the bell schedule fought against it, who modelled learning not as mastery but as wonder. But they did so against a powerful tide. And in too many cases, their work was isolated rather than systemic.

The decline of curiosity isn't just about pedagogy. It's about culture. When schools become places where answers matter more than questions, where efficiency is prized above exploration, and where professional judgment is replaced by scripted delivery, something essential is lost – not just for students, but for educators too. The decline of curiosity isn't just about pedagogy. It's about culture. The spark that drew many teachers into the profession – the desire to learn, to grow, to think alongside others, and to make a meaningful difference in young people's lives – can dim under the weight of conformity. That spark was not just intellectual; it was moral. It came from a deep sense of purpose, a belief that education should expand possibility, not narrow it. When curiosity fades, so too does this moral clarity, replaced instead by procedural compliance and performative routines.

This chapter traces how curiosity slipped from view – not just in classrooms, but in the culture of schools and systems. It argues that curiosity is not a soft skill or a personality trait but a systemic driver of improvement. And it makes the case that bringing it back is not indulgent; it is essential – not only for student learning, but for educator engagement, leadership integrity, and whole-system renewal.

We begin here because without curiosity, improvement becomes a mechanical process: strategies without questions, solutions without wonder, plans without possibility. Curiosity is what allows schools to grow not by replication but by reflection. It is what keeps teaching alive, what makes leadership ethical, and what sustains innovation beyond the cycle of the next policy announcement. It is, as this book argues, the missing engine of educational reform – not in isolation, but as part of a powerful triad alongside moral purpose and school capital.

Bringing curiosity back to the centre of school life won't be easy. It will require shifts in practice, policy, and mindset. But it's not about starting from scratch. The roots are already there – in the student who lingers after class to ask an unexpected question, in the teacher who tweaks a lesson to follow an emerging line of thought, in the leader who begins a staff meeting not with a directive but with an inquiry.

These are not isolated gestures. They are signals. They remind us that curiosity is not gone – it is just waiting for space to grow again. And they form the beginning of a larger argument: that if we want schools to be places of deep, sustained learning, we must make curiosity visible again – not just in words, but in the daily architecture of teaching, leading, and learning.

A system built for certainty

Modern education systems have been shaped by a deep and enduring desire for certainty. Politicians seek clarity – measurable outcomes they can point to in parliament or the media. Parents seek reassurance that their children are progressing, performing, and on track to succeed. Bureaucracies seek control through mechanisms that promise predictability and scalability. In such an environment, curiosity – messy, unpredictable, and slow – is often viewed as inefficient, even threatening. It interrupts timelines, challenges assumptions, and resists simple answers.

Questions take time. They create ambiguity. They invite multiple perspectives and make space for paths not previously considered. For those under pressure to deliver results quickly and visibly, curiosity can seem like an indulgence. But this pressure is not simply cultural; it is built into the machinery of modern schooling. The global education reform movement, as Pasi Sahlberg (2011) argues, has often replaced professional discretion with technocratic control, narrowing the space for local innovation and inquiry.

One of the most visible consequences of this shift is the rise of standardised assessment regimes. In Australia, NAPLAN (National Assessment Program - Literacy and Numeracy) has become both a proxy and a driver for school quality in the public imagination. Although initially introduced as a diagnostic tool to support improvement, NAPLAN results have been increasingly used to rank schools, shape reputations, and guide parental choice (Lingard et al., 2016). This high-stakes framing reshapes how schools operate. It encourages teaching to the test, narrows the curriculum, and privileges easily measured outcomes over more complex or creative learning goals.

Similarly, the senior secondary ATAR (Australian Tertiary Admission Rank) system channels student achievement into a single number that carries immense weight - far beyond its original purpose. For students, that number becomes a proxy for self-worth, success, and future opportunity. The pressure to maximise it can narrow their learning experience to what is assessable and safe. They become strategic rather than curious, risk-averse rather than open (Connell, 2013). For teachers, ATAR pressures often shift pedagogy toward exam preparation and content delivery, reducing space for inquiry, creativity, or deeper engagement. For principals, ATAR outcomes feed directly into school reputation, shaping decisions about subject offerings, staffing, and resource allocation - not always aligned with student wellbeing or equity. And for system leaders, ATAR aggregates are used as performance indicators, informing rankings and policy decisions, sometimes distorting the broader purposes of education.

The reach of ATAR extends even further. In some communities, the perception of a school's ATAR performance weighs heavily on primary school parents, influencing their secondary school choices long before their children encounter formal assessment. The number, though distant, casts a long shadow - shaping expectations, perpetuating competition, and reinforcing advantage.

The result is a culture where each layer of the system - students, teachers, schools, and policymakers - feels the pressure to conform to a narrow metric. Curiosity becomes not just marginalised but actively displaced. The deeper moral purpose of education – to nurture thoughtful, ethical, and engaged citizens – is overshadowed by the pursuit of numerical advantage. The weight of a single number presses down across the system, often at the expense of the very qualities schools aim to foster.

This culture of certainty permeates curriculum design and implementation. The Australian Curriculum, when read in its entirety, is a robust and expansive document. It acknowledges the importance of general capabilities such as critical and creative thinking, ethical understanding, and personal and social capability. However, in practice, these broader aims are often sidelined.

Curriculum implementation, shaped by external pressures, often narrows the scope for inquiry (Lingard & McGregor, 2014) and is mediated by external pressures – school performance measures, parental expectations, and the workload demands on teachers. As a result, many schools fall back on what is safe and visible: ticking off content, following program templates, and preparing students for assessments. Deep inquiry, cross-disciplinary exploration, and reflective learning – hallmarks of a curious classroom – are too often perceived as luxuries rather than essentials.

Vignette: When questions reframe learning

A story of teachers redesigning curriculum to put curiosity back at the centre.

A group of high-performing Brisbane primary schools provides a telling example. Following a combined review of their schools, they undertook a three-year project to redesign curriculum around student inquiry and authentic problem-solving.

The project began after focus groups with Years 3–6 students – attended by educators and parents – revealed a surprising pattern. While the students said they loved their schools, many admitted they were often bored and felt they were being taught things they already knew. For both parents and staff, this was eye-opening.

In response, the schools set out to create a more engaging, inquiry-driven learning experience. They began by identifying broad, enduring questions to spark curiosity and deepen understanding: *How do we live well together? What shapes our environment? How can stories change the world?*

> Teachers co-designed cross-disciplinary units anchored in these questions. Traditional subject boundaries were softened. Assessment practices were reimagined to value questioning, reflection, and growth. Students were invited to pursue their inquiries, test ideas, and share their learning in meaningful ways.
>
> The shift wasn't easy. It required unlearning routines, investing in professional learning, and trusting a less-scripted process. But the impact was profound. Engagement rose. Students saw their learning as purposeful. Teachers reported renewed energy – not just from what they taught, but from the questions they pursued alongside students.
>
> These schools recognised a hidden risk: curiosity sacrificed for coverage, engagement traded for repetition. They chose a different path – one that put curiosity back at the heart of learning.

The cost of curiosity's decline

The decline of curiosity in schools has not gone unnoticed. A growing body of research confirms what many educators have long intuited: curiosity is not a distraction from learning but its very engine. Susan Engel (2011), in her extensive exploration of how curiosity develops in children, argues that the drive to know is both innate and essential. She finds that when classrooms support questioning, exploration, and open-ended investigation, students engage more deeply with content and retain information more meaningfully. Similarly, Todd Kashdan (2009) has shown through psychological research that curiosity enhances attention, persistence, and resilience. It fosters a mindset geared toward learning rather than performance, discovery rather than compliance.

What's more, curiosity doesn't just benefit students. It is also central to effective teaching. Teachers who remain curious – about their students, their practice, and the challenges they face – tend to grow professionally over time. Timperley et al. (2007) emphasise in their best-evidence synthesis of teacher professional learning that taking inquiry into practice is one of the most powerful levers for improvement. When teachers investigate the impact of their strategies, test new approaches, and reflect openly with peers, they become more adaptive, more confident, and more effective.

However, such inquiry-based professional learning often struggles to gain traction in systems that prioritise delivery over discovery. The dominant culture in many education systems is one of implementation. Teachers are given strategies, scripts, and benchmarks – and expected to comply. The opportunity to ask meaningful questions about practice, or to co-construct knowledge with colleagues, is not always embedded in the structure of schools. This leads to what Cochran-Smith and Lytle (2009) term the 'binary of knowledge' – where knowledge is seen as something produced by experts and delivered to practitioners, rather than something generated through professional inquiry. In such systems, curiosity can feel subversive.

The price of suppressing curiosity is steep. For students, the consequences are visible in rising levels of disengagement. According to the OECD's PISA 2018 results, many Australian students report low levels of motivation and a lack of connection between their learning and the real world (Thomson et al., 2020). When students are asked to memorise content without understanding its relevance or invited to regurgitate answers rather than pose questions, their natural inquisitiveness diminishes. The result is a passive form of learning – efficient in appearance, but shallow in impact. Over a century ago, John Dewey warned that when education becomes disconnected from experience and inquiry, it not only fails to inspire but risks becoming miseducative – reinforcing habits of compliance rather than critical engagement (Dewey, 1938). For Dewey, learning was not about acquiring static knowledge but about making sense of the world through active exploration and real-world relevance. In sidelining curiosity and context, we risk denying students the very conditions under which genuine learning takes root.

For teachers, the cost is equally significant. Without space for intellectual exploration and shared inquiry, professional learning can become performative. Teachers may attend mandated sessions or adopt surface-level strategies, but they are not empowered to own their growth. This disconnect between practice and purpose contributes to demoralisation.

Professional capital relies on environments where curiosity is cultivated (Fullan & Hargreaves, 2016) and the combination of human, social, and decisional capital that sustains effective teaching relies on environments where professional curiosity is cultivated. When curiosity is absent, so too is the drive for continuous improvement.

Burnout becomes a serious risk in such environments. Research by Gallup (2014) makes the cost of compliance culture clear: teacher engagement thrives on autonomy, purpose, and professional growth – and withers when these are denied. In systems where teachers cannot exercise judgment, ask questions, or pursue new ideas, the profession itself begins to hollow out. The result? Not just individual burnout, but a collective malaise. Innovation dies. Collaboration turns into box-ticking. The hum of a vibrant staffroom fades to silence. Recent Australian data confirms this trajectory: a 2023 report by the Black Dog Institute found that nearly half of teachers were considering leaving the profession within a year, citing unmanageable workloads, lack of support, and poor mental health. Over 70 per cent reported their workload as unsustainable, and more than half showed symptoms of moderate to severe stress, anxiety, or depression. As Doris Santoro (2018) argues, this is not merely a matter of emotional fatigue, but of demoralisation – a loss of the moral satisfaction that comes from meaningful, ethical work. Teachers feel unable to enact what they believe is good teaching, especially in systems that reduce their role to deliverers of prescriptive content. This demoralisation is now visible in exit intentions, declining morale, and the rising volume of stress-related leave. If the culture of teaching is hollowed out by compliance, so too is the culture of leadership.

At scale, this erosion of professional culture is not a side effect – it is a system failure, undermining the very conditions needed for genuine improvement.

School leaders, too, feel the effects. Under constant pressure to meet targets and manage operations, many principals find themselves drawn into a managerial mindset. Leadership becomes about logistics – budgets, timetables, compliance – rather than about learning. This shift from instructional to operational leadership reduces the space for visionary thinking and shared inquiry. As Hopkins (2007) has argued, managerialism narrows leadership to technical efficiency, crowding out the moral purpose that should underpin educational improvement. Fullan (2003) similarly warns that when school leaders are treated as implementers of policy rather than catalysts of change, leadership loses its connective tissue – its ability to build trust, engage teachers, and foster deep learning cultures. Robinson et al. (2009) found in their meta-analysis that the most effective leaders are those who promote and participate in teacher learning and development. But in systems where curiosity is marginalised and leadership becomes a compliance role, this kind of practice is increasingly difficult to sustain.

The broader impact is felt in reform itself. When schools lose their capacity for inquiry, reform efforts become episodic and superficial. New programs are adopted and abandoned with little learning. Policies are implemented without reflection. Improvement becomes a matter of compliance rather than conviction.

David Hopkins (2020) describes this phenomenon as the 'implementation plateau' – surface-level change without transformation. The system spins, but it does not grow.

Importantly, this is not a failure of will. Educators, by and large, care deeply. They want to make a difference. But they operate in environments that too often fail to reward the dispositions that make real improvement possible: curiosity, courage, collaboration, and critical reflection. These are the very attributes that thrive in conditions of trust, time, and intellectual freedom – conditions that are increasingly rare.

There are signs of hope. Across Australia and beyond, networks of schools are working to reintroduce inquiry into professional learning – through lesson study, instructional rounds, and collaborative inquiry cycles. Teachers are forming research communities and exploring the Scholarship of Teaching and Learning (SoTL) in their own classrooms. Some jurisdictions are investing in practitioner research and evidence-informed innovation. These examples remind us that curiosity, though fragile, is not lost. It remains a renewable resource – one that flourishes when given the right conditions.

To reverse the decline of curiosity, schools and systems must take deliberate steps. This means rethinking how professional learning is designed, how time is allocated, and how success is defined. It means elevating inquiry from the periphery to the centre of school life. And it means recognising that curiosity is not a frill – it is a foundation. Without it, schools become machines. With it, they become communities of learning.

The question, then, is not whether curiosity matters – it clearly does. The question is whether we are prepared to create the conditions in which it can thrive.

The cost of suppressed curiosity – at a glance

Domain	Cost of suppressed curiosity
Students	Disengagement, passive learning
Teaching practice	Reduced professional inquiry, stagnant growth
Teacher wellbeing	Burnout, loss of purpose, decreased autonomy
Leadership	Shift toward managerial leadership, less time for learning
School reform	Compliance-driven initiatives, lack of deep transformation
Professional capital	Erosion of human, social, and decisional capital
Collaboration and culture	Decreased trust, fear of experimentation
System-level impact	Implementation without reflection, innovation stifled

What curiosity really means

To restore curiosity in schools, we first need to understand it – not as a vague feeling or an optional extra, but as a fundamental human drive. Curiosity is not synonymous with interest or engagement. Interest is often passive, a preference for certain topics or activities. Engagement, as defined in many policy documents, can simply mean attention or participation. Curiosity, by contrast, is active and expansive. It is the impulse to explore, to find out, to make sense of something not yet understood. It thrives on uncertainty and resists premature closure. According to Engel (2011), curiosity is not a passive preference but an active, cognitive hunger – an urge to understand, to seek novelty, and to venture into the unknown in search of answers.

Psychologists Todd Kashdan and Paul Silvia (2009) describe curiosity as a multidimensional construct that involves novelty-seeking, openness to new experiences, and a willingness to tolerate ambiguity and complexity. Rather than being a fleeting emotion, curiosity encompasses a sustained drive for meaning. It is both cognitive and emotional, drawing people toward experiences that are challenging, unfamiliar, or unresolved. Curiosity is not about finding the answer quickly – it is about valuing the process of seeking, and being energised by the possibility that something new might be discovered.

In education, curiosity manifests in various ways. It shows up in the questions that students ask when they are encouraged to wonder rather than comply. It appears in the risk a teacher takes when they adapt a lesson mid-stream in response to students' thinking. It surfaces in a school leader's decision to challenge a long-standing policy or investigate a puzzling pattern in student data. Curiosity is a disposition that drives inquiry, reflection, and innovation.

Importantly, curiosity is not a distraction from serious learning – it is where serious learning begins. Engel's (2011) research highlights that when young children are free to follow their questions, they engage more deeply with content and develop stronger cognitive skills. Yet, she also found that most classrooms reward correct answers rather than thoughtful questions. This suggests that many education systems misunderstand how learning actually works. True understanding is not built on answers alone, but on the ability to ask better questions, probe beneath the surface, and revise one's thinking over time.

This view is supported by research from neuroscience and cognitive science. Loewenstein's (1994) 'information-gap theory' proposes that curiosity arises when there is a perceived gap between what we know and what we want to know. This gap generates a feeling of deprivation – an itch to know more – which motivates information-seeking behaviour. In this way, curiosity acts as a bridge between existing knowledge and new learning. It energises attention, boosts memory, and enhances comprehension (Gruber et al., 2014).

Curiosity is also highly relational. It is fostered or diminished by context. In classrooms where questioning is discouraged, where right answers are rewarded and mistakes are penalised, curiosity tends to recede. In contrast, environments that promote intellectual safety, tolerate ambiguity, and invite exploration tend to amplify curiosity. This is particularly important in schools serving disadvantaged communities, where the stakes of failure are higher and the pressure to comply is stronger. Mehta and Fine (2019) argue that when schools reduce learning to narrow metrics, they suppress the conditions in which curiosity can flourish.

For teachers and leaders, curiosity is a professional stance. It means approaching practice with humility and openness. Instead of asking,

'What's the right method?', curious educators ask, 'What's going on here?' or 'Why is this working for some students but not others?' This stance aligns with what Cochran-Smith and Lytle (2009) call 'inquiry as stance' – a view of professional practice that is grounded in ongoing, critical investigation of one's work.

Curiosity is also central to adaptive expertise. Hatano and Inagaki (1986) suggest expert teachers are not those who simply refine known routines, but those who can adapt their knowledge to new situations. This requires curiosity: a willingness to question assumptions, explore alternatives, and respond to complexity. In rapidly changing educational environments – marked by shifting technologies, diverse student needs, and evolving policy contexts – such adaptability is more important than ever.

Moreover, curiosity connects to moral purpose. When educators are curious about their students – their interests, struggles, perspectives – they are better positioned to teach with empathy and equity. When leaders are curious about the experiences of their communities, they are more likely to design policies that respond to real needs. Curiosity, in this sense, is not just a cognitive trait but an ethical one. It pushes educators beyond surface compliance and into a deeper relationship with their work.

And yet, curiosity remains underappreciated in many professional settings. As Kashdan et al. (2004) note, adults are often socialised to suppress curiosity in favour of efficiency or conformity. In schools, this tendency is amplified by pressures to meet benchmarks, implement programs, and maintain order. But if we want schools to be places of learning, we must make space for wondering – not just in students, but in staffrooms and leadership offices as well.

There are promising signs. Some systems are beginning to recognise the role of curiosity in driving school improvement. Inquiry-based learning models, practitioner research networks, and teacher-led innovation projects are all efforts to reintroduce curiosity into the professional landscape. These initiatives remind us that curiosity is not only natural – it is generative. It fuels the cycles of reflection and growth that sustain improvement over time.

To restore curiosity, then, we must treat it not as a luxury but as a core competency. We must build cultures that welcome questions, design structures that support exploration, and protect time for wondering. We must resist the impulse to simplify learning into inputs and outputs, and instead embrace its inherent complexity. Because when we do, we find that curiosity was never truly lost. It was only waiting – for the right conditions, the right questions, and the right people willing to notice and nurture it back to life.

The curiosity-in-schools framework

This framework responds to the growing recognition that curiosity – while often celebrated in rhetoric – is rarely embedded structurally in school improvement efforts. Drawing on research from psychology, organisational learning, and systems reform, it positions curiosity not as a soft skill or individual trait, but as a systemic condition for deep learning, professional growth, and sustainable change.

Level	Manifestation of curiosity	Example
Student	Asking divergent questions; following lines of inquiry beyond the task	A student researching a side-topic not listed in the rubric
Teacher	Adapting lessons based on emerging insights; experimenting with pedagogy	Trialling a new questioning strategy after observing disengagement
Leader	Using data as a springboard for inquiry, not just judgment; co-investigating with staff	Holding a staff dialogue on 'what we're curious about in our teaching'
System	Designing for professional inquiry; valuing reflective metrics over compliance	Allocating time for collaborative inquiry cycles in school improvement plans

This framework is grounded in three key premises:
- **Curiosity is foundational to learning** – for both students and adults. It drives inquiry, engagement, creativity, and persistence.
- **Curiosity is shaped by culture** – It thrives in schools where questioning is valued, risk-taking is supported, and reflection is built into routines.
- **Curiosity must be cultivated deliberately** – through leadership, pedagogy, professional learning, and policy that promote exploration rather than mere compliance.

By articulating curiosity across classrooms, staffrooms, leadership, and system architecture, the framework offers a practical guide for building cultures of sustained inquiry.

Importantly, this is not about inventing something new. In almost every school, the seeds of curiosity already exist – waiting to be noticed, nurtured, and allowed to take root more deeply.

Seeds already planted

Despite the policy constraints, performance pressures, and prevailing narratives of decline, curiosity has not vanished from schools. It persists – not as a systemic norm, but as a stubborn undercurrent, visible in the everyday actions of educators and students who continue to ask, notice, and wonder. Curiosity, in this sense, is not extinct but dormant, waiting in quiet moments for oxygen and space. It lives in the teacher who reworks a lesson to pursue a student's unanticipated line of thinking. It lives in the student who resists the formulaic task and asks instead, 'What if we tried it another way?' It lives in the school leader who treats staff dialogue as inquiry rather than agenda delivery.

These moments are often fragile. They are not enshrined in policies or programs but embedded in relationships and choices. They are acts of professional courage – teachers deviating from the script, students reaching beyond compliance, leaders creating space where uncertainty is welcome. Fullan and Quinn (2016) suggest such actions reflect a deeper culture of learning that cannot be mandated but can be nurtured.

Even in tightly managed environments, educators find ways to preserve pockets of inquiry. A literacy coach might invite a teaching team to co-design an assessment rubric based on observed student misconceptions rather than pre-existing criteria. A science teacher may replace a textbook chapter with an open-ended experiment that prompts students to frame their own questions. A principal may build inquiry time into staff meetings – not as an add-on, but as the core mechanism for school improvement. These practices may seem small or even incidental, but they matter. They are the seeds from which broader cultural shifts can grow.

Importantly, these seeds are not scattered at random. They are often found in schools where leadership protects professional agency, where trust has been built over time, and where the cultural norms of the school endorse rather than punish deviation from the expected. Bryk et al. (2010) argue that the presence of strong relational trust among educators, students, and families is a precondition for deep change. Without trust, curiosity becomes too risky. With it, experimentation becomes part of the learning ecology.

There are also broader movements within the profession that reflect a rekindling of curiosity. The rise of teacher inquiry networks, practitioner research collectives, and peer-led professional learning communities suggests that educators are hungry for more than compliance. They want to think together, to explore ideas, to test possibilities. Projects such as Learning Labs, Spirals of Inquiry (Halbert & Kaser, 2013), and Teaching Sprints (Breakspear & Ryrie Jones, 2021) have all gained traction because they legitimise what many educators already do instinctively: ask questions about practice, test small changes, and reflect on their impact. These structures formalise curiosity – not by prescribing it, but by protecting it.

At the student level, curiosity survives in the interstices of formal schooling. It flourishes during project work, in extracurricular clubs, in interdisciplinary challenges, and in classrooms where dialogue is valued over delivery. Engel (2011) found that when teachers encouraged students to ask their own questions – and treated those questions seriously – student engagement increased, and conceptual understanding deepened. Yet she also noted that such moments were relatively rare, often occurring in loosely structured spaces or outside the formal curriculum. In more tightly regulated environments, the natural inclination to wonder is easily displaced by the push to cover content or meet externally imposed benchmarks.

This view is reinforced in Engel's later work (2015), where she argues that while educators often express support for curiosity in principle, they rarely prioritise it in practice. Many classrooms, she observes, become spaces where questions are infrequent, exploration is constrained, and students are expected to perform more than inquire. As a result, curiosity is pushed to the margins – resurfacing only when conditions allow students the freedom to pursue their interests, experiment with ideas, or learn through genuine discovery.

To reclaim curiosity as a central driver of learning, Engel contends, schools must do more than make rhetorical commitments – they must actively design learning environments that foster questioning, model inquisitiveness, and protect time for open-ended exploration. Without such structural and cultural shifts, curiosity risks becoming an aspirational slogan rather than an educational reality.

The challenge is not that curiosity is absent but that it is unevenly distributed and insufficiently supported. In many schools, these small sparks are isolated from formal improvement efforts. A teacher's pedagogical experimentation might be praised informally but go unnoticed in the school plan. A student's curiosity might be celebrated on a poster but not reflected in assessment practices. Without structural support, these seeds struggle to take root and spread.

Reigniting curiosity requires more than celebrating isolated examples – it demands systematisation without standardisation. Schools need deliberate structures that make curiosity a visible, valued, and integral part of teaching and learning. This might include embedding inquiry into curriculum planning processes, making time for co-inquiry among staff, or revising assessment policies to honour process over product. It may also involve rethinking leadership models to prioritise listening, noticing, and stewarding professional dialogue.

Crucially, this work must also be equity-centred. Too often, the conditions that allow curiosity to flourish are more available in high-SES (socioeconomic-status) schools, where accountability pressures are perceived to be lower and professional autonomy is higher. In disadvantaged schools, by contrast, the pressure to 'cover content' and meet performance benchmarks can lead to a narrowing of the learning experience. As Mehta and Fine (2019) note, deeper learning – and the curiosity that fuels it – should not be a privilege for the few, but a right for all.

To shift this dynamic, schools and systems must move beyond the rhetoric of curiosity as enrichment and embed it as a core function. This means elevating professional trust, encouraging intellectual risk-taking, and designing for wonder – not just once a term, but every day. It also means recognising and resourcing the informal networks where curiosity already thrives.

Professional learning initiatives that start with teachers' questions, rather than imposed content, are more likely to generate engagement and improvement (Timperley et al., 2007).

Ultimately, the seeds of curiosity are already present in almost every school. The question is not whether curiosity exists, but whether we choose to notice it, nurture it, and scale it. Doing so requires courage, design, and belief. It requires us to see inquiry not as a special event but as the default stance of learning communities. It demands that we treat questions – not just answers – as the lifeblood of education.

Vignette: A primary school, a question, and a language reclaimed

A story of how one student's question sparked cultural and curriculum change.

In a primary school tucked into Melbourne's northern suburbs, a teacher named Eleni begins a unit on the history of First Nations peoples. The curriculum materials offer a timeline, a few Dreaming stories, and a list of key events. The class begins dutifully enough – students copying notes and matching dates. But then a boy, Joel, raises his hand: 'Why don't we speak the languages that were here first?'

The question lands awkwardly. The teacher hesitates. There is no space for this on the scope-and-sequence. But it lingers in the room. Later that day, she raises it at a team meeting. One colleague shares that a local Aboriginal education group, the Victorian Aboriginal Education Association, has offered to support schools introducing language programs.

Eleni goes back to her principal, and together they begin asking questions. What would it take to honour that offer? Could they start with just one word a day? Could a local Elder visit?

Within a term, the school launches a modest Indigenous language program. It begins with acknowledgments of Country spoken in both languages. It grows into weekly lessons that weave language with culture and story. Students start asking different questions. Some start researching the Country their families live on. One class writes a letter to the local council asking for dual naming of streets and parks.

It's a small beginning – unmeasured, unmandated, and invisible in the performance reports. But something shifts. Not just in curriculum, but in culture. A question made it possible. And a space for curiosity – protected and pursued – allowed it to grow into change.

Yet such stories remain the exception rather than the norm. Across too many classrooms and staffrooms, the slow erosion of curiosity continues to take a quiet but measurable toll – on learners, on teachers, and on the very capacity of schools to renew themselves.

The way back

Bringing curiosity back means changing more than pedagogy. It means shifting the culture of schools and the assumptions of systems. It requires rethinking what matters in education – not just the content we deliver, but the mindset we model and the habits we cultivate. It means resisting the pull of urgency long enough to ask: What kind of learning are we really fostering? Are we teaching students to seek certainty, or to explore possibility?

This shift is not cosmetic. It calls for a deeper reconsideration of how schools are organised, how teachers are supported, how leadership is enacted, and how success is defined. Cultivating curiosity means creating space for questioning – space in the timetable, space in the curriculum, space in the relationships between students and teachers, between teachers and leaders. It means slowing down to reflect, even in the face of fast-moving demands. And it means reimagining the role of the teacher, not as a transmitter of information, but as a cultivator of thinking. Nearly a century ago, Dewey (1938) reminded us that education should awaken minds, not merely fill them.

This book argues that curiosity, moral purpose, and school capital are not peripheral to school improvement – they are its foundation. They are not 'nice to have' values to be appended to strategic plans; they are the core elements that make real and lasting improvement possible. When curiosity is re-centred, schools begin to look and feel different. They become places where learning is not only delivered, but discovered – by students and teachers alike. Where improvement is not only planned, but pursued with shared intent. Where teachers don't merely implement – they investigate. Where leaders don't just set targets – they ask better questions. Where people do not simply work – they wonder.

To bring curiosity back is also to bring back meaning. Systems built on compliance eventually hollow out the very practices they intend to standardise. In contrast, systems built on trust and inquiry allow professionalism to flourish. Teachers regain their sense of agency. Students re-engage with learning, not because they must, but because it matters. Leaders rediscover the power of dialogue and reflection over directive and control. These are not abstract aspirations. They are the everyday outcomes of cultures that make curiosity visible, valued, and actionable.

Importantly, none of this happens in isolation. A curious classroom depends on a curious teacher.

A curious teacher thrives in a curious school. A curious school is sustained by a curious system. The conditions must align. That alignment is the work of leaders, policymakers, and practitioners alike – not in imposing uniformity, but in protecting the space for diverse and rigorous inquiry to take root.

And the payoff is not just better test scores or more efficient processes. The payoff is a learning environment where students become critical thinkers, adaptable problem-solvers, and lifelong learners. Where teachers feel professionally alive, connected to purpose and possibility. Where schools serve not just as institutions of instruction, but as communities of curiosity and hope.

From insight to action: reclaiming curiosity in school improvement

What might it mean to reawaken curiosity in your setting?

These provocations and practical entry points are designed to help schools move from insight to implementation – gently, collectively, and with purpose.

For teachers:

- **Notice the patterns:** Where in your week does curiosity flourish – and where does it fade? Consider a curiosity journal or team discussion to uncover what enables or suppresses inquiry.
- **Try a small pivot:** Start one lesson with a genuine puzzle or provocative question. Let students' questions drive the next step.
- **Defer the outcome:** Replace one answer-focused activity with a process-focused one. Prioritise exploration over solution.

For leaders:

- **Audit the culture:** What's the emotional climate in staff meetings or planning sessions? Are questions welcomed or rushed past?
- **Protect time for wondering:** Schedule a standing 'What are we noticing?' agenda item in leadership or team meetings.
- **Challenge the language:** Shift from 'accountability' talk to learning talk. Try swapping 'Have they met the benchmark?' with 'What do we understand now that we didn't before?'

For systems:

- **Rethink performance signals:** Are your frameworks rewarding curiosity and growth, or just delivery and certainty?
- **Celebrate inquiry:** Recognise and share examples of genuine questioning, adaptive practice, and risk-taking – even if outcomes aren't perfect.
- **Slow down before scaling up:** Give schools space to learn, reflect, and iterate before demanding replication.

The goal is not to implement a checklist but to rekindle a stance. Curiosity begins not with a structure, but with a disposition. The rest will follow.

The Curious Cat, after all, was never truly gone. It had simply retreated to the quiet corners, the overlooked moments, the back pages of lesson plans. It was waiting – patiently, provocatively – for someone to notice the question it left behind. And now, perhaps, it is time to follow it – not with certainty, but with openness. Not with answers, but with better questions. Because in the end, that is how transformation begins – not with a mandate, but with a moment of wonder.

Afterword: an invitation to notice

This first chapter began with a quiet loss – the fading of something once so embedded in the life of schools that we barely noticed it until it was gone. Curiosity, once a natural current beneath our classrooms and staffrooms, has become an elusive presence: visible in moments, but no longer central to how we think, teach, lead, or improve.

But naming its absence is not an act of nostalgia. It's a call to action.

If schools are to be places of transformation – not just transmission – we need to remember what curiosity makes possible. It invites depth. It disrupts complacency. It dares us to learn, even when we are meant to already know. And it reconnects us to the reason many of us came into education in the first place: a belief in growth, a faith in potential, and a commitment to the flourishing of others.

The first step in any renewal is not strategy. It is recognition. Curiosity, though sidelined, has never disappeared. It lives in the quiet courage of teachers who tweak a lesson because a student asked a better question. It lives in the leader who pauses before responding, to really listen. It lives in the willingness of a system – or an individual within it – to say, 'What if there's another way?'

That is where this book begins: with a question, not an answer. The chapters that follow explore how curiosity lives within moral purpose and school capital – how it threads through teaching, leadership, equity, and system design. They argue that improvement is a matter not only of structure or pressure, but of culture – and that culture begins with what we notice, what we value, and what we make time for.

The next chapter looks outward – at the broader system landscape – and asks why school improvement itself has stalled. In doing so, it begins to frame how curiosity, moral purpose, and school capital might offer a way forward.

So the first question is this: In our school, where is curiosity alive? Where has it been quietly waiting? And what might happen if we made space for it to lead?

And somewhere in the corner of the system, the Curious Cat watches still – its tail flicking, its gaze steady – wondering why so much improvement has stalled, and what might yet be possible if we remembered how to ask.

CHAPTER 2
School Improvement Has Stalled

BIG IDEAS IN THIS CHAPTER

Reform fatigue is real. Waves of initiatives, frameworks, and compliance pressures have left educators weary and systems fragmented.

The promise of improvement has often failed to deliver – not from lack of effort, but because of incoherence between policy intent and classroom reality.

Standardisation and technocratic models have crowded out professional judgment, creativity, and shared moral purpose.

Stalled improvement is not inevitable. It's a signal that deeper change is needed – change rooted in culture, not control.

This chapter asks:

- Why has school improvement stalled?
- What kind of shift might restore purpose, trust, and progress?

'You don't need a weatherman to know which way the wind blows.'
– Bob Dylan

Vignette: The principal's dilemma

A story of how one school leader wove curiosity, culture, and community into the heart of learning.

The pressures that stall improvement are not abstract; they live in the daily choices educators must make – between covering the curriculum or creating space for meaning, between compliance and connection. The story of one Melbourne principal offers a glimpse of what it takes to resist those pressures and lead with curiosity and moral purpose.

When Jack became principal of a small, culturally diverse primary school in Melbourne's northern suburbs, he knew he'd need to focus on raising academic achievement and strengthening community trust. What he hadn't anticipated was a deeper challenge – one that would test not just his leadership skills but his sense of purpose.

The school had a growing number of Aboriginal students, but beyond a daily Acknowledgment of Country, there was little visible recognition of culture or Country in classroom life. At a local gathering early in his tenure, an Elder posed a question that stayed with him: 'Do your kids know whose land they're learning on?'

Jack brought the question back to his staff. Some responded with cautious curiosity. Others were hesitant. 'We barely have time to get through the basics,' one teacher said. 'And I wouldn't know where to start.' The leadership team was split. Would introducing an Indigenous language and culture program be seen as a distraction from 'core business'? Would parents support it? Would staff have the confidence to do it well?

Jack decided to lead with listening. Building on the work of his predecessor, he strengthened relationships with local Aboriginal educators and community members. Gradually, a proposal emerged: to introduce a Woiwurrung language program alongside a broader inquiry into place, history, and cultural identity. It wasn't mandated. It wasn't part of a compliance cycle. But it felt right.

The early months were uneven. Some staff worried about 'getting it wrong'. Others embraced the opportunity with humility and care. A few parents questioned whether it was necessary. One even asked if the school was 'being political.'

But over time, things shifted. Students who had often been disengaged began to participate with pride. Teachers wove cultural inquiry across the curriculum. Conversations deepened. In later years of the endeavour, the entire school community joined a local march in support of the Truth Commission's findings – a key part of Victoria's treaty process. For many, it was the first time they had connected their learning with real-world justice.

NAPLAN results did not decline. In fact, student engagement, attendance, and wellbeing indicators began to rise. James hadn't set out to improve the data – but the data, like the culture of the school, began to tell a new story.

In staff meetings now, Jack no longer asks, 'How can we fit this in?' He asks, 'How can we not?'

Jack's story is not unusual in its challenges – but it is increasingly rare in its response. While many schools are caught in cycles of compliance, his school found a path back to purpose. This chapter explores why such paths are so hard to sustain – and how systems might make them easier to walk.

The fact that Jack's school had to carve out this work against the grain of the system – rather than through it – speaks volumes. In too many schools, the question is still 'How can we fit this in?' rather than 'How can we not?' The system is not yet designed to nurture this kind of learning. Until it is, improvement will remain fragile and uneven – dependent on exceptional leadership, not normalised practice.

A tired reform cycle

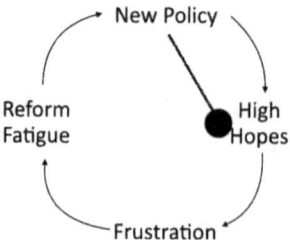

Education reform, once full of promise, now often feels like déjà vu. Teachers and leaders trace a familiar cycle: new policy arrives, professional development follows, strategic plans are rewritten, metrics are introduced, and enthusiasm briefly lifts. But soon after, routines resume, competing initiatives pile up, and students see little change in daily learning. The reform wheel spins, but the terrain stays the same.

> Reforms have rolled across schools in waves for more than a century. Yet below the surface, in the classrooms where teachers teach and students learn, the sea is often calm and the life of schools goes on much as before. (Cuban, 1990, p. 4)

Cuban's 30-year-old observation remains painfully relevant. Despite grand cycles of reform, teaching and learning remain stubbornly consistent. This isn't due to poor intent – many reforms are research-based and carefully articulated – but because they're often conceived far from classrooms and implemented through compliance, not curiosity. Teachers experience them as burdens, not enablers. Fatigue sets in – not from change, but from change that fails to connect.

This repetitive cycle breeds scepticism. Educators tire of silver bullets. They see slogans change, but the pressures remain. This isn't cynicism, but cautious hope. Experienced teachers want reform that's coherent, contextual, and connected to real classroom work. In time-poor environments, they invest in what lasts, not what's fleeting. As one principal said, 'We've seen it all before. If we wait long enough, it'll swing back again.'

Too often, reforms focus narrowly on literacy and numeracy scores, sidelining broader learning and wellbeing. The result is reductive teaching – 'teaching to the test' – that sacrifices engagement and creativity. The irony:

in trying to raise standards, we often diminish the very conditions students need to thrive.

Most reforms don't address the cultural fabric of schools. They tinker with curriculum or assessment but ignore the relational and organisational dynamics that shape collaboration. Without cultural coherence, even strong strategies stumble. As Fullan (2011) notes, system change requires both structure and culture.

David Hopkins (2024) echoes this in *Unleashing Greatness*. He warns against over-reliance on compliance models, calling instead for inquiry-driven leadership and investment in professional capital. True improvement, he argues, stems from empowered practitioners and adaptive cultures – not rigid implementation.

Dean Ashenden (2024) likens stalled systems to 'beached whales' – stranded by their own bulk. Bloated policies, rigid accountability, and a lack of adaptability leave many schools trapped in an architecture no longer fit for purpose.

In this context, improvement has stalled – not from apathy, but because the system clings to novelty while ignoring necessity. What's needed isn't another initiative, but a shift in mindset. Real improvement starts not with rollout plans but with curiosity, moral purpose, and shared capital.

And just beyond the reach of the latest policy document, the Curious Cat is watching – waiting for someone to ask a different question.

The implementation trap

The second sign of stalled improvement is the increasingly familiar pattern of implementation without transformation. Across systems, governments launch new strategies, back them with investment and political rhetoric, and roll out timelines, frameworks, and toolkits. Yet too often, these result in surface-level shifts rather than deep change. Much of this reflects what Alan Reid (2019) calls 'thin change' – visible and reportable, but not enduring.

This is not unique to Australia. Across OECD countries, systems are proficient at initiating change, but far less effective at embedding it. Policymakers point to milestones and progress markers. Yet for educators, the experience is often one of constant adaptation without consolidation. Policies land loudly but rarely take root. Schools respond through passive compliance – updating plans, attending training – while continuing to work around familiar realities.

A major cause is the pace and proliferation of reforms. Many policies are replaced within three to five years – before their impact can be properly evaluated. Schools remain in a kind of permanent beta mode: implementing one initiative while bracing for the next. David Hopkins (2024) notes that sustainable change depends not on how many reforms are launched but how much learning is sustained. He points to weak or inconsistent embedding of foundational conditions – clear theory of action, leadership development, and capacity-building. Without these, reforms drift above the culture of schools. Meanwhile, teaching, shaped by historical structures, still struggles to build a robust professional culture grounded in inquiry and research. Bureaucratic mindsets often dominate – prioritising accountability over learning.

This helps explain the fatigue many educators feel – and the erosion of professional conditions where curiosity and innovation might thrive. Systemic change requires more than launching programs; it requires cultivating the deep habits and shared purpose needed for schools to think, reflect, and grow over time.

The implementation trap is both structural and cultural. The divide between policy design and school practice has widened. Even well-intentioned reforms are filtered through accountability lenses, stripping them of creative potential and replacing agency with oversight.

This is most acute where trust is low. Strategic plans may speak of empowerment or innovation, but if teachers experience reforms as top-down mandates, the message rings hollow. They comply outwardly, but privately feel frustrated and disengaged. As one principal put it: 'Give it 18 months and the pendulum will swing again.'

This isn't apathy. It's self-preservation. Educators want to improve, but they know real change comes from clarity, community, and purpose – not rollout plans. Reform lacks power without connection.

Reform is never neutral – it lives in emotion and relationship. Teachers bring histories, values, and hopes to the work. If they feel disillusioned or over-scrutinised, even well-designed strategies falter. Culture, not compliance, drives deep change.

One of the casualties is professional learning. It becomes transactional – sessions delivered, modules ticked off. But genuine growth arises from dialogue, inquiry, and trust. These flourish in schools that value curiosity over compliance.

To break the trap, system leaders must resist the allure of speed and scale. Focus on what matters: student learning, teacher agency, and school culture. Hold that focus long enough for practice to embed. Think of reform not as delivery but as development. This means fewer programs, more conversation. Fewer dashboards, more trust.

And it means reconnecting with purpose. Educators invest in what they believe in. Without moral clarity, initiatives drift. When purpose is clear, and curiosity invited, schools become more than implementers – they become learners.

Reform that sticks starts with listening – not just to surveys, but to cultural signals: Where are people asking real questions? Where is inquiry thriving? Reform grounded in these places feels lived, not laminated.

The Curious Cat, if it could speak, might remind us: meaningful change begins not with an announcement but with a question – a question asked by someone who is ready to listen.

Misalignment between policy and practice

The third signal that school improvement has stalled is the persistent disconnect between policy intent and educational reality. This misalignment isn't just about communication gaps or weak implementation; it's a structural problem born from reforms developed at a distance from classrooms.

Too often, policies are designed in agencies or advisory circles without involving those who do the actual work – teachers, leaders, and students. As a result, they may be technically sound but culturally tone-deaf. When reforms roll out, educators are asked to buy in to ideas they had no part in shaping. Engagement becomes superficial. Uptake, minimal.

This disconnect creates tension. Teachers experience cognitive dissonance between their values and what they're being asked to do. Leaders juggle system demands with staff wellbeing. Students are caught in environments shaped more by data goals than learning needs. Improvement feels imposed, not inspired.

Worse, many of the metrics used to track success only amplify the problem. Standardised test scores and attendance rates can obscure more meaningful indicators of progress – engagement, growth, belonging. Schools chase numbers, often at the cost of curiosity and relevance. This goal distortion means that what is measured overrides what truly matters.

None of this is to say policy is irrelevant. Many reforms are well-founded. But unless schools are involved in shaping and adapting those reforms, their impact is shallow. As Fullan and Gallagher (2020) argue, coherence arises through shared meaning – not just alignment on paper.

A more productive model would treat educators as co-designers, not implementers. That requires time, trust, and dialogue. It also demands system investment in professional capital – so that teachers are equipped not just to deliver change but to think critically and shape it.

Where policy and practice align, schools feel different. Teachers speak with ownership. Leaders act with confidence. Students see their learning connected to something that matters. These are not fantasy schools – they exist. But they exist because the system made space for curiosity and collaboration to thrive.

The Curious Cat would find such places irresistible. Not because they're perfect, but because they're alive. They are shaped by questions, not compliance – by a culture that values listening over listing. If misalignment signals a stall, reconnection is how we get moving again.

The culture problem: when trust erodes

Beyond repetition and thin implementation lies a deeper concern: the erosion of trust. As reforms accumulate and expectations grow, the emotional climate of schools shifts. Educators who entered the profession with a sense of vocation now find themselves working within a culture that can feel procedural and transactional. The result isn't just fatigue – it's a loss of meaning.

This is no minor glitch. It's a systemic cultural issue. When educators experience reform as something done to them, their professional agency diminishes. As Berliner (2006) and Darling-Hammond (2010) argue, teaching is intellectual and relational. It requires moral clarity as much as technical skill. Without trust, that clarity dims.

In Australia and globally, centralised accountability has carried a cultural cost. Risk aversion and constant scrutiny have become default settings. Too often, schools are shaped by narratives of crisis and deficiency. In response, policymakers roll out urgent fixes – tougher standards, mandated programs, compliance mechanisms. But the cumulative effect is what Stephen Ball (2003) calls 'a culture of surveillance', where performance is audited and educators feel constantly evaluated.

Instead of trusting schools to improve through inquiry, reforms often default to control. Public narratives fuel this by framing education as broken and in need of rescue. While politically expedient, these stories are pedagogically corrosive. Scott Eacott (2017) describes them as 'performativity cultures', where narrow indicators define success and improvement becomes more about appearances than authentic growth.

In these settings, teachers resort to strategic compliance – doing enough to meet expectations without engaging deeply. Innovation gives way to caution. Professional learning becomes a requirement, not a resource. Data becomes a performance, not a dialogue. Classrooms lose their vibrancy.

Leaders, meanwhile, straddle competing pressures. They must translate system priorities – often tied to funding and public image – while nurturing cultures of shared learning and trust. It's an emotionally demanding balancing act.

The deeper irony is that systems often say the right things. They champion agency, innovation, and student voice. But without trust, time, and tolerance for risk, those ambitions stay rhetorical. NAPLAN's high-stakes use narrows curriculum and discourages inquiry (Hardy, 2015). Autonomy initiatives like Independent Public Schools often add administrative load without real empowerment (Gobby, 2013). Even initial teacher education reforms risk casting teaching as compliance, not judgment (TEMAG, 2015).

Coherence, Fullan and Quinn (2016) remind us, grows from shared ownership – not just aligned documents. Rebuilding trust requires sustained investment in autonomy, collaboration, and culture. It means supporting schools to lead improvement from within – not as a rejection of accountability, but as a recognition that deep change depends on those closest to the learning.

There are hopeful signs. Where schools foster teacher inquiry, distribute leadership, and protect time for collaboration, cultures begin to shift. Trust grows not from declarations, but from signals that expertise is valued. Systems can support this by reducing reform churn, strengthening relationships, and modelling the learning they expect from schools.

Ultimately, this is a relational issue. The ties between educators, communities, and leaders shape the conditions for improvement. Without attention to these dynamics, even the best reforms falter. Palmer (1998) reminds us that good teaching comes from identity and integrity – not technique. That identity thrives in cultures of dignity, respect, and trust.

Renewing that culture isn't fast. It requires unlearning habits of fear and rebuilding habits of inquiry and shared purpose. It requires leaders who prioritise long-term learning over short-term metrics.

And so, the Curious Cat peers into the staffroom – not for binders or posters, but for the real clues: Is there laughter? Are there questions? Is there room for disagreement and imagination? Because in those moments, more than in any strategy document, lie the conditions from which real change can grow.

New coordinates for a different map

If school improvement has stalled, it's not because educators lack care or capacity – it's because the prevailing model has run its course. For years, reform agendas have leaned on structure, speed, and measurement. They've chased quick wins through frameworks, audits, and mandates.

But delivery isn't development, and compliance doesn't yield commitment.

To move forward, we need a different set of coordinates – ones anchored in professional trust, moral clarity, and a revival of curiosity.

This doesn't mean abandoning accountability. It means reframing it. What are we holding schools accountable for? Are we measuring what matters – or just what's easy to count? Are we creating space for teachers and leaders to think deeply and act purposefully? As Hannon and Mackay (2023) argue, systems must evolve from delivery to learning cultures – for students and adults alike.

That evolution begins with purpose. When purpose is taken seriously, it offers coherence and direction. Without it, reform becomes fragmented – checklists, audits, slogans. With it, schools align action with values. As Fullan and Quinn (2016) note, clarity of purpose inspires more than compliance ever could. When educators connect to a shared 'why', they persevere through challenge and complexity.

The second coordinate is professional capital. Hargreaves and Fullan (2012) define this as the human expertise of teachers, the social bonds of collaboration, and the decisional judgment honed through practice. Reform needs to invest in all three. That means recruiting well, supporting growth, and building cultures of shared inquiry. It means treating teacher knowledge as something generated in context – not just delivered from outside.

Professional learning, in this view, isn't training – it's thinking. It's collaborative, contextual, and often messy. The most effective schools carve out time for shared reflection. They welcome challenge. Their leaders don't just monitor – they facilitate growth.

The third coordinate is curiosity. Often overlooked in reform discourse, curiosity is the spark that drives inquiry and renewal. It invites the question 'What else is possible?' It shifts schools from defensive routines to explorative ones.

Curiosity isn't fluff. It energises thinking, drives innovation, and helps schools navigate complexity. Systems that value it protect time for joint work, encourage experimentation, and reward reflection. In these cultures, questions aren't distractions – they're the starting point.

Taken together, purpose, capital, and curiosity form a different kind of map. It won't guarantee linear progress. But it offers a direction that's intellectually honest and emotionally sustainable. It allows for coherence without conformity. It gives space for human judgment to flourish.

On the ground, this map looks like co-constructed learning, question-led staff meetings, and inquiry-rich classrooms. It looks like leaders who invite dialogue, and systems that invest in trust. It looks like permission to think.

This isn't the end of reform – but it is the end of reform as a checklist. What lies ahead is slower, deeper, and more human.

And just beyond the edges of the latest strategy document, the Curious Cat stretches – ready to chase the next good question.

From insight to action: reclaiming school improvement

If school improvement has stalled, don't reach for a new plan – reach for new questions, clearer purpose, and stronger culture. These actions help shift the work from episodic initiatives to enduring, inquiry-driven change.

For school leaders:

- **Reconnect with purpose:** Revisit your school's 'why' – what are we really here to achieve, and how do we know when we're moving toward it?
- **Audit initiative overload:** What are we doing because it matters, and what are we doing because it was mandated? Make space by letting go.
- **Start a listening campaign:** Hold structured conversations with staff, students, and families to learn how improvement is experienced – and where it's felt most.
- **Reframe professional learning:** Shift from delivery to dialogue. Create space for educators to explore, question, and co-design.

For educators:

- **Surface the invisible:** In team meetings, ask: 'What parts of our practice are we doing out of habit, not impact?'
- **Look for bright spots:** Find small examples of meaningful learning, even in tough contexts. Use them as anchors for further change.
- **Challenge the script:** Replace 'That won't work here' with 'What would make that possible in our setting?'

For systems and networks:
- **Invest in trust-building infrastructure:** Facilitate peer observation, inquiry networks, and cross-school sharing – not just compliance checks.
- **Decentralise wisdom:** Tap into what schools already know. Use system data to support, not direct.
- **Be wary of silver bullets:** Focus on coherence, culture, and capability – slow work that lasts.

If we want to move beyond the stalled cycles of reform, we must first build the conditions where purposeful, inquiry-rich cultures can grow – from the classroom to the staffroom to the system as a whole.

Afterword: when the dust settles

If reform has felt exhausting, it's because we've been running at the wrong pace – chasing quick fixes when what's needed is slow thinking and deep listening. The problem is not a lack of ideas or urgency. It's a lack of alignment between what we say we value and how we actually work.

This chapter has argued that the future of school improvement lies not in the next program, policy, or dashboard, but in restoring the conditions that allow learning to flourish – for students and adults alike. That means putting moral purpose, professional capital, and curiosity back at the centre of our efforts – not as add-ons, but as anchors.

The next chapter turns to the first of these anchors – moral purpose – and explores how it provides the steady rhythm that can reconnect improvement work with its deepest values.

We don't need another revolution. We need a recalibration – a rebalancing of our educational ecosystems so they become places of inquiry, not just implementation. So they honour the craft of teaching and the intelligence of those who do it. So they nourish rather than deplete.

Somewhere near the edge of this conversation, the Curious Cat lingers – not just watching, but waiting. Waiting for a system brave enough to follow the questions again. To choose learning over labelling. To trust curiosity as the first, not the last, act of real reform.

CHAPTER 3

Moral Purpose and the Rhythm of Reform

BIG IDEAS IN THIS CHAPTER

Moral purpose is the heartbeat of authentic school improvement. It gives reform ethical grounding and enduring relevance.

Good work in education requires more than technical skill – it demands moral clarity, professional agency, and deep commitment to students and equity.

Without moral purpose, change becomes performative, short-lived, or misaligned with learners' needs.

Reform that lasts moves in rhythm, not in bursts. It honours cycles of reflection, adaptation, and re-commitment.

This chapter asks:

- What does moral purpose look like in action?
- How can it guide leaders, systems, and teachers in turbulent times?

> *'We each have a responsibility to make the world a better place –
> bit by bit, small gesture by small gesture.'* – Nick Cave

A school is more than its buildings, budgets, or benchmarks. At its core, it is a community shaped by purpose. When that purpose is strong, shared, and ethically grounded, schools become places not just of instruction but of transformation. Moral purpose is not a lofty ideal – it is the guiding force behind the everyday decisions educators make: how they respond to a child in need, design a task, lead a team, or navigate setbacks.

In systems often preoccupied with performance, compliance, and competition, moral purpose offers a different rhythm – one grounded in service, care, and equity. It steadies practice when reform feels chaotic and energises learning when fatigue sets in. More than a slogan, it's a compass – a directional force that animates schools with intention and coherence.

Michael Fullan (2003) describes moral purpose as 'acting with the intention of making a positive difference in the lives of students' (p. 29). This is not an add-on to leadership or teaching – it is their foundation. Without a clear sense of why we educate, schools risk becoming efficient but hollow. With it, even the most constrained environments can become places of possibility.

Howard Gardner, Mihaly Csikszentmihalyi, and William Damon (2001) describe this ethical dimension through their concept of 'Good Work' – work that is excellent in quality, socially responsible, and personally meaningful. Their triad of excellence, engagement, and ethics underscores the demands placed on educators. Sustained improvement depends on the interplay of all three.

Crucially, moral purpose is not solitary. It thrives in community. Hargreaves and Shirley (2009) suggest that moral purpose gains momentum when it is shared and enacted collectively. It is expressed not only in strategic plans or public statements, but in daily conversations, staffroom culture, rituals, and routines. It is shaped by leadership, supported by colleagues, and sustained by the stories schools tell themselves about who they are – and who they serve.

Defining moral purpose

Moral purpose in education is the commitment to making a positive difference in the lives of all students – especially those who are marginalised or underserved. It is the ethical driver that elevates teaching from the delivery of content to the shaping of lives.

It also anchors reform efforts in something more enduring than policy cycles or performance pressures. It reminds educators and systems alike that the ultimate goal is not simply to improve test scores or meet benchmarks, but to ensure that every student – regardless of background – has access to the opportunities, relationships, and challenges they need to thrive.

Importantly, moral purpose is relational. It gains momentum when shared and enacted collectively – a dynamic explored in depth by Hargreaves and Shirley (2009). In this view, moral purpose is not merely espoused in mission statements or strategic plans; it is enacted in staff meetings, classroom interactions, hallway conversations, and leadership decisions. It becomes part of the school's lived culture – reinforced through rituals, protected through structures, and deepened through dialogue.

Leaders play a vital role in cultivating and sustaining moral purpose. Leithwood and Riehl (2005) suggest effective school leadership involves not just managing operations but 'developing people' and 'setting directions'. Leaders who prioritise moral purpose attend not only to outcomes but to the processes and relationships through which those outcomes are achieved.

A key feature of morally purposeful leadership is its commitment to equity. It recognises that not all students begin from the same starting line, and that treating everyone the same does not guarantee fairness. Equity, according to Fullan and Quinn (2016), involves 'ensuring that all students are equipped to pursue their aspirations' (p. 33) and that schools take deliberate action to remove systemic barriers to learning.

Yet moral purpose is not invulnerable. In environments dominated by standardisation or compliance, it can become diluted or displaced. Schools may lose sight of their core purpose, defaulting instead to what is expedient or externally mandated. That is why moral purpose must be protected and renewed. It cannot be assumed – it must be cultivated, shared, and sustained.

This renewal often begins with reflection. It might be a question posed at a staff meeting: 'What brought you to this work, and what keeps you here?'

It might be a collaborative review of the school's improvement plan, asking whether current strategies align with the school's values. Or it might be the decision to foreground student voice in curriculum planning. These moments help reconnect educators with the moral dimensions of their role.

In times of uncertainty, moral purpose acts as an internal compass. It guides decision-making when data is incomplete, when resources are stretched, or when pressures are conflicting. 'Moral purpose is not a luxury – it is a necessity,' reminds Fullan (2011, p. 35). It ensures that schools remain human places, driven not just by performance but by principle.

Moral purpose as a contested concept

While moral purpose is often described in noble terms – service, equity, transformation – it is not a universally agreed-upon idea. What one educator views as a moral imperative, another might experience as a distraction or even an ideological imposition. In contemporary education, moral purpose is increasingly framed through divergent lenses: some see it as raising academic standards and preparing students for a competitive global economy; others locate it in student wellbeing, cultural inclusion, environmental sustainability, or social justice. These views are not mutually exclusive – but they can come into tension, especially when values collide or resources are limited (Biesta, 2020).

In day-to-day practice, these tensions emerge in dilemmas that require ethical navigation. Should a school prioritise data-driven instruction to meet achievement benchmarks, or prioritise inquiry-based learning that fosters creativity and voice? Should wellbeing programs centre on clinical interventions or community healing? Should curriculum decisions reflect national standards or local community values? These are not only practical decisions – they are moral ones, shaped by what educators believe matters most and for whom (Gale & Parker, 2017).

These differing views are also shaped by positionality. Policymakers may emphasise system performance, drawing on narrow definitions of success based on test scores and graduate pathways. Teachers may prioritise relational work with students, especially in communities facing trauma, marginalisation, or poverty. Families may place different weight on cultural identity, inclusion, or academic advancement. Even among school leaders, understandings vary – some rooted in a commitment to equity and redress, others in a belief in excellence and meritocracy. Fischetti and Keddie (2021) have observed that school leadership is increasingly shaped by conflicting pressures: performativity, compliance, ethical care, and the politics of inclusion.

Acknowledging these tensions does not weaken moral purpose – it makes it stronger. To assume that moral purpose is self-evident or uncontroversial is to ignore the realities of contested educational landscapes. Education is inherently value-laden (Biesta, 2020): it's not simply about how we teach, but about what we teach for – and why. Without this deeper reflection, there is a risk that moral purpose becomes either rhetorical – slogans without substance – or hegemonic, imposing one worldview at the expense of others.

Instead, schools need to engage in purposeful dialogue that surfaces assumptions, debates priorities, and seeks ethical coherence. This does not mean consensus on every issue, but it does require shared reflection on guiding values. For example, one school might foreground moral purpose in terms of advancing Indigenous reconciliation, investing in language programs and truth-telling initiatives. Another might frame moral purpose around tackling entrenched disadvantage through rigorous literacy instruction. Both can be valid. What matters is that each school articulates a vision anchored in its community, rather than adopting abstract or imposed definitions (Lampert, 2022).

Leaders play a critical role here. They are not just stewards of systems, but custodians of purpose. Gobby and Mockler (2022) noted that the complexity of school leadership today demands not only strategic agility but moral depth. Leaders must navigate ambiguity, mediate competing demands, and build a culture where ethical reflection is part of everyday professional life. This includes asking difficult questions about whose voices are amplified, whose values are privileged, and what kind of futures schools are preparing young people for.

Recognising moral purpose as contested also means being open to critique. Too often, moral language is used to shut down rather than open up discussion. Terms like 'excellence' or 'equity' can become empty signifiers unless unpacked and debated. A genuinely inclusive moral purpose requires schools to 'sit with discomfort' and engage with difference – not as a box to tick, but as a call to transformation (D'warte & Slaughter, 2023).

Yet moral purpose, like curiosity, can be co-opted or diluted. In many education systems, the language of equity, inclusion, and 'every child succeeding' is now ubiquitous. Mission statements ring with purpose. But when this moral purpose is not grounded in daily practice, deep relationships, and ethical reflection, it becomes performative – a veneer of virtue rather than a driver of authentic improvement. This kind of *surface purpose* may even mask the persistence of inequity beneath the rhetoric. Policy language alone, Sahlberg (2016) warns, does not shift classroom realities. The challenge for leaders and systems is not just to articulate moral purpose, but to embody it – visibly, relationally, and with courage.

In this light, moral purpose is not a finished product. It is an evolving conversation – shaped by context, contested by perspective, and enriched by reflection. The more honestly that conversation is held, the more likely schools are to build cultures that are not only technically effective but ethically grounded. It is in this daily, dialogic work that moral purpose becomes real – not a distant aspiration, but a compass for decision-making, culture-building, and improvement.

The interplay of moral purpose, curiosity, and school capital

Moral purpose does not operate in isolation. It gains traction and transformative power when it intersects with two other forces: curiosity and school capital. Together, these elements form the cultural and intellectual infrastructure of a learning system that is both equitable and future-oriented. While moral purpose provides direction, curiosity supplies the energy, and school capital ensures the capacity for change.

Curiosity, as explored in earlier chapters, is the drive to explore, inquire, and understand. In education, it fuels the professional learning of teachers, the reflective leadership of principals, and the engaged questioning of students. But curiosity on its own – ungrounded in purpose – can be diffuse or even misdirected. It is the ethical clarity of moral purpose that shapes curiosity into disciplined inquiry: exploration that is not just novel, but necessary.

Research on workplace curiosity supports this connection. Kashdan et al. (2020) argue that curiosity in adults is more than a disposition; it is a skill that can be cultivated and directed toward productive ends. In education, this means teachers and leaders who not only ask questions but ask the right questions – those that challenge inequity, interrogate assumptions, and reimagine practice. Curiosity becomes a tool for transformation, not just a personality trait. When moral purpose anchors that curiosity, it leads to inquiry that matters.

But inquiry, even with purpose, requires supportive conditions to thrive. This is where school capital plays a vital role. Building on the work of Hargreaves and Fullan (2012) and extended by Caldwell and Harris (2008), school capital refers to the accumulated resources – intellectual, social, organisational, and financial – that enable improvement. These are not just inputs; they are dynamic assets that grow through purposeful use.

Intellectual capital includes the professional knowledge and pedagogical skill of teachers, supported by continuous learning and evidence-informed practice. Social capital involves the trust, collaboration, and shared norms within a school community that enable collective problem-solving. Organisational capital refers to the structures and routines that make innovation possible – such as time for collaboration, data protocols, or distributed leadership. Financial capital, while often externally constrained, becomes potent when aligned with strategic priorities that reflect the school's moral purpose.

When schools invest in these forms of capital, they create the conditions for moral purpose and curiosity to interact. A curious teacher is more likely to engage in inquiry if they have time to collaborate (organisational capital), access to new ideas (intellectual capital), and colleagues they trust (social capital). Similarly, a leader with a strong moral compass can only turn that intention into action if the school's capital allows for flexibility, learning, and experimentation.

This dynamic was evident in a school leadership initiative launched in Victoria's northern suburbs, where improvement efforts were guided by three core principles: being literate, numerate, and curious. Schools were not told how to achieve these goals, but were supported through peer coaching, inquiry-based professional learning, and collaborative planning. Over time, the interaction of moral purpose (a commitment to equity and excellence), curiosity (a willingness to question and learn), and capital (resources and structures to support change) created a culture of trust and shared improvement. NAPLAN scores improved – but more importantly, so did professional morale, student engagement, and family partnerships.

The research on effective schools reinforces this interplay. As Hopkins (2024) argues in *Unleashing Greatness*, lasting system change arises not from mandates or measurements alone, but from the alignment of purpose, inquiry, and enabling conditions. When curiosity and moral purpose are embedded within schools rich in capital, improvement becomes more than technical – it becomes cultural.

However, when any of these elements is missing, improvement stalls. A school with strong moral purpose but limited capital may become exhausted, its aspirations outpacing its capacity. A school rich in resources but lacking purpose may drift or default to compliance. And a school that encourages curiosity but fails to connect it to ethical aims may become distracted or fragmented. The key lies in integration – seeing these forces not as separate levers but as interdependent dimensions of a healthy learning system.

This integrated view challenges dominant narratives about reform. It suggests that improvement is not a series of isolated interventions, but a process of cultural cultivation. It asks policymakers to design systems that support not just technical delivery but human flourishing. And it invites educators to reclaim the language of purpose and inquiry – not as idealistic extras, but as essential elements of the work.

Ultimately, when curiosity and moral purpose operate within well-capitalised schools, they generate momentum that extends beyond individual classrooms. They shape the culture of the school, influence its partnerships with families and communities, and contribute to a profession that feels both intellectually alive and ethically grounded.

In such schools, improvement is not imposed – it is grown. It emerges from the interplay of aspiration and inquiry, structure and spirit. And while there will always be challenges, the presence of moral purpose ensures that those challenges are faced with clarity, courage, and care.

It is here, in the convergence of curiosity, capital, and moral clarity, that the deepest and most enduring school improvement occurs.

Leading with moral purpose: from intention to coherence

While moral purpose may feel personal, in schools it is also political and collective. It involves navigating competing values, systemic pressures, and social expectations – because education is never neutral. Every decision about priorities, support, and leadership reflects broader debates about equity, excellence, and the role of schooling. Moral purpose doesn't live in mission statements – it must be enacted, modelled, and sustained daily.

This work falls heavily on school leaders, who are not just operational managers but custodians of purpose. Their decisions shape how moral purpose is understood, protected, and lived across the school.

Leadership for moral purpose means creating environments where the right things are easy to do – a point emphasised by Fullan (2003). This goes beyond articulating values; it means aligning systems, structures, and relationships around those values. A principal who talks about equity but protects poor teaching practice undermines trust. A leader who espouses collaboration but rewards individualism weakens the collective. Cultivating moral purpose is not a matter of intention – it's a matter of coherence.

Coherence begins with clarity. Leaders must help their communities define what they mean by moral purpose, and why it matters. For some schools, this might focus on equity for disadvantaged students. For others, it might mean lifting the engagement of all learners or strengthening character and citizenship. What matters is not that every school adopts the same vision, but that each one develops a vision that is shared, understood, and anchored in local reality (Sharratt & Fullan, 2012).

This process is most effective when it is dialogic, not imposed. Rather than delivering a pre-written vision to staff, leaders can facilitate processes where teachers, students, and families help shape the school's moral compass. This might include reflective workshops, collaborative storytelling, or data-driven conversations that surface the school's aspirations and contradictions. The goal is to build shared language – and shared ownership.

Beyond articulation, moral purpose must be embedded into daily practice. Leaders need to signal, through their routines and rituals, what really matters. This includes how time is allocated (is there time for joint learning?), how success is defined (are we celebrating growth, not just grades?), and how feedback is given (are we naming moral courage as well as technical skill?).

Leaders can also embed moral purpose by focusing on what Ron Berger (2003) calls 'beautiful work' – learning that is authentic, challenging, and tied to real-world impact. When students produce work that matters, it affirms their agency and reaffirms the school's commitment to meaningful learning. Leaders who showcase this work – through exhibitions, student-led conferences, or storytelling – strengthen the cultural narrative that learning has moral weight.

Another key leadership strategy is to protect and elevate moral courage. In every school, there are moments when doing the right thing is harder than doing the easy thing – when a teacher challenges deficit assumptions, when a team rethinks a problematic behaviour policy, when a leader confronts underperformance not out of blame but out of deep care for students. These moments often go unnoticed, but they are the heartbeat of moral purpose. Leaders who name and honour them send a powerful message: this is who we are.

Crucially, leaders must also model the discomfort that moral purpose sometimes requires. 'Leadership is not about being the hero of your own story. It's about being the host of other people's growth,' write Hargreaves and Shirley (2009). This means acknowledging mistakes, inviting feedback, and staying open to learning. Moral purpose is not perfectionism – it is a commitment to continual ethical reflection and improvement.

Professional learning is a key lever in this work. As Timperley et al. (2007) have shown, professional learning is most impactful when it is embedded in inquiry, linked to student outcomes, and sustained over time. Leaders can use professional learning not just to build skills but to deepen moral discourse. For example, a session on formative assessment can include not only technical strategies but a discussion of what it means to treat feedback as a right, not a reward. A meeting on reading data can explore not just targets but what literacy means for student dignity and future opportunity.

Structures matter too. Leadership teams should align improvement plans, staff goals, and performance processes with moral purpose. This includes ensuring that appraisal conversations include time to reflect on ethical goals, not just technical benchmarks. It also includes using student voice and family perspectives as part of evaluative processes – not as token gestures, but as moral counterweights to system pressure.

The power of these approaches lies not in any single act but in their accumulation. Over time, a school that takes moral purpose seriously begins to feel different. Conversations deepen. Decisions slow down. Courage shows up. And while tensions remain – between equity and excellence, autonomy and alignment, care and accountability – they are approached with greater thoughtfulness.

Importantly, moral purpose should never be used as a shield against critique or a mask for managerialism. Schools can – and should – be held accountable for student learning and wellbeing. But they must also be held accountable for how they pursue these goals. A school that achieves academic success by silencing student voice or eroding teacher autonomy has missed the point. Cochran-Smith and Lytle (2009) maintain that inquiry and equity must go hand-in-hand.

In systems that often feel rushed, reactive, and reductive, moral purpose offers a different rhythm. It invites leaders to slow down, to centre relationships, to name what matters, and to build cultures that last beyond the tenure of any one person. It is not a utopian ideal. It is a grounded, disciplined practice.

And perhaps, just outside the office door, the Curious Cat waits – curled beside a staffroom conversation about a struggling student, or peering over the shoulder of a teacher rewriting a unit to better reflect students' identities. The Cat doesn't pounce. It observes, it listens. Because it knows that in every act of moral clarity, another seed of lasting improvement is sown.

Yet sustaining moral purpose is not simply a matter of vision or intention. It is a question of rhythm – of how the deeper pulse of ethical commitment is paced and protected within the relentless tempo of school life.

Aligning the rhythms of school life and moral purpose

Every school moves to two rhythms: one fast and visible, the other slow and deep (Hopkins & Craig, 2016). The rhythm of reporting cycles, compliance deadlines, and public accountability often sets the pace. But beneath it runs the quieter rhythm of moral purpose – trust, care, reflection, and growth. Aligning these rhythms is the work of wise leadership.

When moral purpose is strong, it helps align these rhythms. It ensures that the fast-paced demands of the calendar don't override the deeper pulse of ethical improvement. It reminds leaders that real change doesn't happen in a term – it happens over years, through coherence, care, and commitment.

Without this alignment, schools risk chasing reform on the surface while standing still underneath. The noise of strategy drowns out the music of purpose. But when rhythms align – when a school's daily actions are guided by enduring moral commitments – then reform stops feeling like a storm and starts to feel like a tide: powerful, patient, and deeply transformative.

Vignette: A disconnect between values and practice

A story of how competing system pressures eroded a school's commitment to care and connection.

At a large metropolitan secondary school, the leadership team launched a bold new vision: 'Every student known, valued, and supported.' Posters with the slogan appeared in corridors, staff handbooks, and even student diaries. The principal spoke often about wellbeing and equity, citing a commitment to inclusive learning and trauma-informed practice. Staff were initially energised. Many had long felt that academic pressures had overtaken care and connection.

Yet as the year progressed, tensions began to surface. Teachers were directed to reduce student referral numbers – even when behaviour was severely disruptive – because suspensions would affect the school's performance review. Specialist wellbeing roles were reduced as a result of budget realignment. Time for pastoral meetings was cut to make room for additional NAPLAN preparation. Professional learning sessions once devoted to restorative practice were sometimes replaced with sessions on compliance with new data-entry protocols.

By the end of the year, staff morale had plummeted. Teachers felt torn between their professional judgment and system metrics. 'We talk about valuing every student,' one staff member observed, 'but we're spending more time entering behaviour codes than actually talking to kids.'

The school's stated moral purpose remained unchanged. But in practice, it had been hollowed out by external mandates and internal contradictions. What began as an inspiring vision had become a source of cynicism. The gap between words and actions widened – and trust eroded.

This experience is not unique. What the teachers in this school encountered was not a lack of commitment – it was a form of what Doris Santoro (2018) calls *demoralisation*. Unlike burnout, which suggests emotional depletion, demoralisation stems from the inability to enact one's professional values within a system that constrains or contradicts them.

Teachers still care deeply, but the structures around them make it difficult – sometimes impossible – to do what they believe is right for their students. In such circumstances, moral purpose is not lost but thwarted, hollowed out by systemic contradictions and procedural demands. When teachers are asked to prioritise data entry over relationships, or compliance over compassion, the result is not just frustration – it is ethical harm. And over time, if unaddressed, it leads to withdrawal, disillusionment, or departure.

Part of the problem was a failure to recognise and reconcile the different rhythms at play. The rhythm of school life – with its urgent timelines, accountability pressures, and procedural churn – had overtaken the slower, steadier rhythm of development, where trust, relationships, and moral purpose take time to grow. When these rhythms fall out of sync, even the most well-intentioned reforms can collapse under the weight of performative urgency. Real improvement, as Hopkins and Craig (2016) suggest, depends not just on clarity of vision, but on coherence of tempo.

From insight to action: moral purpose and the rhythm of reform

Moral purpose is not a slogan – it's a rhythm we return to. These prompts invite teachers, leaders, and system partners to reflect on how that rhythm is expressed, protected, and sustained in their daily work.

For teachers:

- When have I felt most aligned with my moral purpose in the classroom?
- Are there moments when I've chosen safety over what I know is right for learners?
- How do I talk with colleagues and students about what matters – and why?

For school leaders:

- What signals do we send about what really matters in our school?
- Do our improvement efforts reflect a clear, shared moral purpose – or compliance with external expectations?
- How do we handle difficult conversations – with clarity, with compassion, and with purpose?

For systems:

- Are we creating space for moral reflection – not just strategic execution?
- How do we recognise and protect educators who act with integrity, especially under pressure?
- Are we building reform agendas around what matters – or what's measurable?

However we define improvement, its heartbeat must be moral purpose – steady, shared, and strong enough to sustain us through complexity and change. It is this shared compass that enables curious, courageous, and compassionate schools to thrive.

Afterword: the compass in our hands

Moral purpose is not a slogan for school walls. It is the compass we carry in the quiet moments – when we face a difficult decision, when we stand up for a child others have written off, when we keep going after the third knockback or the fifth attempt to shift a stuck practice. It is easy to talk about values when times are smooth. The test is whether they hold when things get hard.

In every school, the ethical core is tested daily. Will we prioritise what's measurable over what's meaningful? Will we excuse low expectations in the name of empathy? Will we accept poor-quality teaching from a colleague out of misplaced loyalty or fear of conflict, even when students are being short-changed? Will we make space for staff to grow or demand quick wins for the sake of optics? These questions cannot be answered by policy – they require judgment, integrity, and deep moral grounding.

This chapter has argued that moral purpose is more than a personal trait. It is a shared, cultural commitment that must be enacted and sustained through leadership, relationships, and systems. When schools get this right, they become more than sites of learning. They become communities of care and conviction – places where excellence and equity are pursued together, not as trade-offs but as dual imperatives.

The next chapter explores the conditions that help this moral purpose take root and grow – through the development of school capital in all its dimensions.

And if, in the middle of all this, you notice a tail disappearing around the corner or a small pair of eyes watching quietly from the windowsill, don't be alarmed. The Curious Cat hasn't wandered far. It knows that where there is moral clarity, curiosity will soon follow.

CHAPTER 4
School Capital – The Conditions for Growth

BIG IDEAS IN THIS CHAPTER

School capital is what makes improvement possible. It's the combination of intellectual, social, organisational, and financial resources that enable change to take root.

Capital is unevenly distributed – within and between schools. Recognising this is essential to designing fair, effective strategies for improvement.

Strong capital allows schools to move from intention to action. Without it, even the best ideas struggle to gain traction.

Building capital is a collective task. It grows through trust, collaboration, shared learning, and purposeful investment – not just top-down reform.

This chapter asks:

- What is the state of our capital?
- What do we need to grow in order to support deeper, more sustained improvement?

'You just have to look, it's always been here.' – Charles Jenkins

The work of school improvement is not just about what we add, but what we notice and nurture. Much of what makes schools thrive is already present, waiting to be seen and strengthened. This chapter explores the forms of school capital that give learning its shape and strength.

Why capital matters: the hidden infrastructure of improvement

School improvement is often framed around actions: new programs, revised policies, evidence-based strategies. But beneath every successful change effort lies something less visible and far more enduring – school capital. While outcomes tend to get the headlines, it is the conditions that enable those outcomes that truly determine whether change is possible, let alone sustainable.

School capital refers to the resources, relationships, and routines that schools draw upon to learn, adapt, and improve. It is the hidden infrastructure of improvement – the foundation that supports everything from pedagogical shifts to leadership development. When school capital is strong, innovation can take root. When it is weak or uneven, even the most promising initiatives struggle to gain traction.

The term draws on the influential work of Brian Caldwell and Jessica Harris (2008), who argued that educational reform too often focuses on surface-level interventions without investing in the deep reservoirs of capacity that schools need to enact and sustain change. They proposed that school capital is not a single thing, but a constellation of interacting forces: intellectual capital (the knowledge and expertise of people), social capital (the quality of relationships and networks), organisational capital (the structures and routines that enable coherence), and financial capital (the resources that support the work). When these forms of capital are aligned and developed deliberately, schools become more resilient, more innovative, and more equitable.

Yet capital is often taken for granted. Policies may assume that schools already have the internal capacity to implement change, without recognising the vast differences in capital between schools in low-SES (socioeconomic-status) communities and those with more structural advantages. In my research, schools with strong moral purpose and high levels of workplace curiosity made only limited progress in improving student learning unless school capital was present as an enabling condition. This reinforces Caldwell and Harris's contention that capital is not merely a background factor – it is a core determinant of improvement.

Understanding capital also helps explain why change efforts sometimes succeed in one school but fail in another. It's not always the strategy that differs – it's the readiness. Two schools might adopt the same literacy framework or coaching model, but their results will diverge depending on the strength of their professional trust, the time they have for reflection, the quality of their internal dialogue, and the availability of skilled facilitators. These are not peripheral considerations. They are the difference between performative implementation and meaningful learning.

Framing school capital as a system of conditions rather than a set of fixed assets also invites a different approach to leadership. Rather than focusing only on external mandates or top-down targets, leaders can ask: 'What's the current state of our school capital? Where are the gaps? What can we grow?' Improvement, in this framing, is less about pushing programs and more about investing in the soil – so that what is planted has a chance to take root and flourish.

This chapter explores each dimension of school capital in turn. It draws on theory and lived experience to show how schools build, strengthen, and sometimes lose the enabling conditions for change. It also shows how the four capitals intersect – and how their synergy can accelerate improvement when aligned to a shared moral purpose. As we'll see, school capital is not just about capacity. It's about confidence, continuity, and the collective will to improve.

Understanding this hidden infrastructure begins with the most foundational layer of capacity: the knowledge and expertise that educators bring to their work – and how that knowledge is grown and shared.

Intellectual capital: knowledge as a lever for change

At the heart of every school lies its most vital resource: the professional knowledge, expertise, and insight of its people. Intellectual capital refers to this collective capacity – the depth and quality of what educators know and can do, individually and together. It includes pedagogical content knowledge, curriculum understanding, assessment literacy, and the ability to respond to diverse student needs. But more than that, it encompasses the habits of mind and learning dispositions that enable educators to keep growing.

When intellectual capital is strong, a school is better able to analyse its challenges, respond with purpose, and refine its practice. When it is weak or uneven, improvement becomes fragile – dependent on individuals rather than embedded in the culture. As David Hargreaves (2001) argued in his influential work on knowledge-creating schools, innovation emerges when professional knowledge is not only held but shared and built collaboratively. A single expert teacher can lift outcomes for one class. But a strong culture of intellectual capital can lift a whole school.

Building intellectual capital requires more than sending teachers to workshops or providing access to content. It depends on the creation of shared spaces where professional learning is embedded in practice – where staff routinely examine student work, observe one another, analyse data together, and reflect on the impact of their teaching. These habits turn knowledge into a living system, not a static storehouse.

One secondary school in regional Victoria, for example, created 'discipline hubs' across curriculum areas where teachers met fortnightly to bring student work samples, identify areas of cognitive demand, and co-design new tasks that stretched thinking. The goal was not compliance with a framework, but the activation of pedagogical thinking. Over time, this led to greater alignment of high-impact strategies across the school and a marked improvement in student engagement and growth. More importantly, it strengthened the belief among staff that their collective knowledge was powerful – and worth investing in.

Intellectual capital also thrives when inquiry becomes a routine feature of teacher practice. When educators are encouraged to ask questions – 'What's working? What's missing? What am I assuming?' – and to pursue answers collaboratively, they strengthen not only their practice but their professional identity. Helen Timperley and colleagues (2007) emphasised this in their best evidence synthesis on professional learning: teachers deepen their expertise when they are supported to investigate, reflect, and refine in iterative cycles, rather than being passive recipients of externally designed solutions.

A powerful insight from my thesis also reinforces this point: in schools with higher levels of workplace curiosity, intellectual capital was more likely to be shared and mobilised. In other words, curiosity created the conditions for knowledge to flow. Teachers who were encouraged to wonder, reflect, and test ideas were also more likely to contribute to a collective knowledge base. Intellectual capital, then, is not simply a stockpile of expertise – it is a dynamic system powered by curiosity and trust.

Importantly, this form of capital is cumulative. As schools invest in the intellectual growth of their staff – through coaching, mentoring, collaborative planning, or peer observation – they build a more agile and confident workforce. New teachers benefit from the wisdom of experienced colleagues. Leaders benefit from multiple perspectives on practice. Students benefit from deeper, more responsive teaching. And over time, the school becomes more than the sum of its parts.

But intellectual capital is also vulnerable. High staff turnover, burnout, narrow accountability measures, and time poverty can erode it quickly. Schools that do not protect time for professional learning, or that prioritise delivery over reflection, risk turning teaching into a technical exercise rather than a professional craft. And when the flow of knowledge stalls, so too does improvement.

For this reason, the development of intellectual capital must be intentional. It must be resourced, scheduled, and celebrated. Leaders must ask: 'How are we helping staff learn? Where are the knowledge gaps? How do we ensure that learning is shared, not siloed? And how do we recognise the value of pedagogical dialogue – not just as a support function, but as a driver of innovation?'

Yet knowledge alone is not enough. For intellectual capital to become a force for school-wide improvement, it must flow – through relationships of trust, reciprocity, and shared purpose.

Social capital: trust, reciprocity, and shared purpose

If intellectual capital is about what people know, **social capital** is about how they connect. It refers to the quality of relationships within a school – the trust between colleagues, the flow of information across teams, and the shared norms that underpin collaboration. Social capital enables knowledge to move. It is what allows a good idea in one classroom to become a shared strategy across many.

Social capital is built through repeated interactions, mutual respect, and a shared commitment to student learning. It grows when teachers feel safe to admit uncertainty, when teams have structures for meaningful dialogue, and when leaders model openness and empathy. Without social capital, even the most capable staff can become isolated. But with it, **collective efficacy** emerges – the belief that, together, we can make a difference.

This collective belief is not merely sentimental. John Hattie's (2008) meta-analyses highlight collective teacher efficacy as one of the most powerful influences on student achievement. Yet this efficacy does not emerge spontaneously – it is constructed through relationships. It is in the informal conversations after a lesson, the shared struggle with a challenging class, the co-planning of an unfamiliar unit. These moments, while easily overlooked, are the threads from which strong school cultures are woven.

In my own leadership practice, I have seen the catalytic power of social capital in schools that move from fragmentation to cohesion. In one newly merged primary school, early resistance and fractured staff morale were gradually transformed through a consistent focus on shared inquiry. The principal deliberately paired staff from different legacy schools for co-teaching and mentoring roles. Weekly 'learning huddles' were introduced – short, informal conversations where teachers brought one wondering question about their practice and explored it with a colleague. Over time, trust deepened. As one teacher put it, 'We stopped defending our classrooms and started opening them.'

Social capital also enables the transfer of intellectual capital. A school might have deep expertise in a particular strategy or curriculum area, but unless there is trust and willingness to share, that knowledge remains siloed. Relationships act as conduits. They allow professional learning to travel – across grades, across departments, and between leadership and staff.

The matrix below illustrates how the interaction between intellectual and social capital shapes a school's capacity for collective improvement.

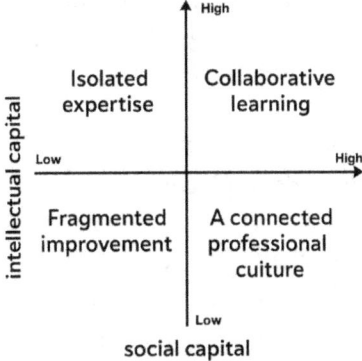

Each quadrant represents a different cultural and instructional profile:

Quadrant 1: Fragmented improvement with low intellectual capital and low social capital

- School learning culture: Isolated, underdeveloped, and disconnected.
- Professional environment: Staff often work in silos. Professional dialogue is rare or surface-level.
- Outcomes:
  - Limited professional growth
  - Minimal collaboration
  - Low collective efficacy
  - Change efforts are sporadic and short-lived
  - School improvement is stalled or non-existent.

Quadrant 2: Isolated expertise with high intellectual capital but low social capital

- School learning culture: High individual knowledge but lacking collaboration or shared trust.
- Professional environment: Strong individual practice, but expertise remains trapped in classrooms.
- Outcomes:
  - Talent is under-leveraged
  - Little diffusion of best practice
  - Innovation is inconsistent and unsustained
  - Potential is high, but impact is low due to lack of connectivity
  - Teacher burnout risk may be elevated.

Quadrant 3: A connected professional culture but with low intellectual capital and high social capital

- School learning culture: Warm, collegial, and relationship-rich.
- Professional environment: Strong collaboration, but often lacks rigour or depth in teaching and learning.
- Outcomes:
  - Harmony is valued over growth
  - Risk of groupthink or complacency
  - Professional learning may be superficial
  - Limited gains in student achievement
  - High morale but low instructional traction.

Quadrant 4: Collaborative learning with high intellectual capital and high social capital

- School learning culture: Intellectually rich and relationally strong; a dynamic learning culture.
- Professional environment: Educators share expertise, engage in rigorous dialogue, and co-construct knowledge.
- Outcomes:
  - High-impact professional learning
  - Strong collective efficacy
  - Sustainable school improvement
  - Innovation spreads and sticks
  - Student learning thrives in a culture of shared growth.

This matrix reinforces the principle that capital is not just about individual assets – it's about shared conditions. When intellectual and social capital align, schools move beyond pockets of excellence to cultures of sustained, distributed improvement.

Bryk and Schneider's (2002) seminal research in Chicago schools demonstrated that relational trust among educators is a key predictor of school improvement. In schools with high trust, teachers were more likely to innovate, collaborate, and persist through difficulty. In low-trust schools, even well-funded reform efforts struggled to gain traction. Trust, in this sense, is not soft – it is strategic. It shapes the emotional climate in which all other forms of capital operate.

Importantly, social capital also includes external relationships. Schools that are well-networked – with other schools, community organisations, universities, or professional associations – can tap into broader knowledge systems. This form of boundary-crossing extends learning and avoids the insularity that can breed stagnation.

But as with other forms of capital, social capital is not evenly distributed. In schools marked by historical division, high staff turnover, or toxic cultures, trust can be eroded. It takes deliberate leadership to rebuild it – and time. Structures help: protocols for dialogue, norms for meetings, space for collaborative planning. But what matters most is consistency. As trust builds, so does the willingness to take risks, share practice, and stretch thinking.

Social capital is ultimately the connective tissue of improvement. It is the web that holds learning together, ensuring that what is known becomes what is shared – and what is shared becomes what is possible.

Organisational capital: coherence, routines, and distributed leadership

Relationships and knowledge thrive when they are supported by coherent structures. Organisational capital provides the routines and systems that enable learning to become collective and sustainable.

Organisational capital refers to the structures, routines, and systems that support and sustain improvement. It's the way a school organises itself to learn – how it schedules time, distributes leadership, communicates priorities, and embeds expectations. While intellectual and social capital focus on people, organisational capital focuses on the enabling environment in which those people work. Done well, it holds learning together. Done poorly, it fragments effort and stifles initiative.

At its core, organisational capital is about coherence. As Fullan and Quinn (2016) argue, coherence is not achieved by aligning every detail, but by cultivating clarity of purpose and direction. When staff know what matters, why it matters, and how their work connects to it, they are more likely to act with confidence and creativity. Incoherence, on the other hand, breeds confusion, compliance, and fatigue.

However, coherence can easily tip into control. Routines that were introduced to support collaboration can become rituals of compliance. Timetables designed to protect professional learning can be crowded out by layers of mandatory reporting. Improvement frameworks can become overloaded with templates and tick-box tools, dulling curiosity and narrowing reflection. When organisational capital drifts toward bureaucracy, it risks suppressing the very inquiry and agency it was meant to enable. This is particularly true in schools under high accountability pressure, where the line between structure and surveillance can blur. Leaders must remain alert to this drift. As one middle leader put it, 'We had time to meet, but not to think.' Strong organisational capital creates scaffolds, not scripts. It should clarify the work, not choreograph it.

In one metropolitan secondary school, the leadership team introduced a three-week inquiry cycle for faculty teams. Each cycle began with a shared question drawn from schoolwide data, followed by co-planning, classroom observation, and reflection. These routines gave shape to professional learning, but they also created momentum. Teachers knew when and how they would engage in inquiry, and they trusted that it wasn't going to be replaced with a new initiative every term. As one teacher put it, 'We finally stopped chasing improvement and started building it.'

Organisational capital also enables distributed leadership. It ensures that responsibility for improvement is not confined to the principal or a handful of middle leaders, but shared across teams and roles. In schools with strong organisational capital, leadership is seen not as a position, but as a practice – something that can be grown, coached, and activated in others. This builds resilience. It means that when one leader leaves, the culture of inquiry continues.

Importantly, organisational capital must support – not stifle – curiosity. The goal is not to add layers of structure, but to design conditions in which people can think, experiment, and learn. Routines can serve this goal only if they are held lightly, reviewed regularly, and adapted to purpose. Structures should evolve in response to learning, not constrain it.

The School Improvement Tree metaphor – introduced in detail later in the book – captures this well. If moral purpose is the root system and school capital is the trunk, then organisational capital is like the cambium layer—a thin, active band just beneath the bark where structural growth happens. It generates the wood and bark that keep the tree strong and upright. In schools, this is the routines, systems, and structures that support learning and improvement. And like the cambium, it needs attention, adjustment, and care to stay healthy and effective.

Structures should help people look up and outward – not down and inward.

In practice, this means asking questions like: 'Are our meeting agendas aligned with our improvement priorities? Do our timetables allow for meaningful collaboration? Are staff roles designed to support professional growth, or simply to manage compliance?' These are not operational details. They are cultural signals. They show staff what really matters.

Many schools fall into the trap of initiative overload – layering program upon program without the routines or reflection time to integrate them. Organisational capital is the antidote to this. It creates the patterns and rhythms that make professional learning stick. These might include structured inquiry cycles, weekly collaborative planning time, instructional leadership teams, or transparent processes for reviewing practice. The point is not bureaucracy. It's clarity. It's knowing that improvement is not a one-off event, but a sustained conversation built into the fabric of the school.

As we turn next to financial capital, it becomes clear that organisational coherence is not just about what schools do – it's about what they enable. Strong systems don't just manage complexity – they create the space in which curiosity, collaboration, and care can thrive.

Structures and routines, however, do not operate in a vacuum. They depend on resources – time, staffing, and funding – that must be used flexibly and wisely. Financial capital shapes what is possible.

Financial capital: equity, flexibility, and enabling conditions

Behind these structures lies the reality of resourcing. Financial capital, wisely used, provides the time and flexibility schools need to protect inquiry, enable collaboration, and respond to complexity.

Financial capital is often the most visible form of school capital, but also the most misunderstood. It refers not only to how much funding a school receives, but how flexibly it can use that funding to enable improvement. In effective schools, financial capital is not treated as a budget to be spent – it is treated as a lever for learning. It is strategically deployed to build the intellectual, social, and organisational capacities that sustain change.

The reality, however, is that financial capital is unevenly distributed across Australian schools. Despite equity-focused policies such as the Gonski funding reforms, large gaps remain between schools in low-SES communities and their higher-SES counterparts – not just in per-student funding, but in access to discretionary resources, community support, and philanthropic investment (Lamb et al., 2014). These financial gaps translate into significant differences in opportunity: the ability to hire specialist staff, release teachers for collaboration, maintain safe and modern facilities, or invest in sustained professional learning.

In my research, schools with limited financial capital often struggled to protect time for inquiry or implement promising initiatives, even when staff had strong moral purpose and professional will. Leaders spoke of constantly 'robbing Peter to pay Paul' – juggling staffing and program costs in ways that undermined continuity. Conversely, schools with targeted financial support – particularly when paired with autonomy – were able to create the enabling conditions for sustained change.

Flexibility is key. It's not just how much money a school has, but what it is allowed to do with it. Too often, funding is tied to narrow metrics or short-term accountability cycles, limiting schools' ability to invest in long-term capacity-building. Curious schools use financial capital to fund time: for teachers to collaborate, for leaders to coach, for teams to learn together. They also invest in roles that support relational and instructional depth – such as inquiry leads, EALD mentors, or trauma-informed practitioners – recognising that improvement is relational as much as technical.

A compelling example comes from a cluster of schools that pooled resources to create a series of regional school improvement networks. Each school contributed a portion of its professional learning budget to fund a network coordinator, release time for peer observation, and shared access to visiting academics. What began as a modest collaboration became a powerful source of energy and expertise. Within two years, the schools reported increased student engagement, stronger teacher retention, and greater alignment of pedagogical practice – all catalysed by strategic investment of financial capital.

Financial capital also signals priorities. When schools allocate resources to inquiry, collaboration, and wellbeing, they are not just funding activities – they are expressing a theory of change. Conversely, when funding is diverted into compliance-heavy reporting tools, or consumed by one-off consultant programs with limited follow-through, it can send a message that reflection and relationship matter less than performance optics.

At the system level, this raises important questions. What kinds of spending build capital? How do funding models support curiosity, equity, and sustained professional growth? And how might policies be redesigned to trust schools to use their financial capital wisely, not just efficiently?

The best use of financial capital is not to purchase silver-bullet solutions – it is to create the time, space, and stability for educators to do their best work. This includes ensuring that the most challenged schools have not only the funding but the trust to direct it toward what they know will make a difference.

As we'll see in the next section, the real power of capital lies in its interconnection. Financial capital on its own cannot drive improvement – but when it is used to build intellectual, social, and organisational strength, it becomes a powerful catalyst for change.

But while thoughtful investment can catalyse growth, it is also constrained by systemic factors beyond any one school's control. Acknowledging these constraints is essential if we are to build capital equitably.

Systemic constraints and uneven access to capital

While this chapter highlights the importance of building school capital from within, it's critical to acknowledge that not all schools begin from the same starting line. Systemic constraints – such as funding models, staffing policies, accountability regimes, and geographic isolation – create significant disparities in how easily capital can be developed or sustained. These constraints are particularly acute in low-SES schools, rural and remote settings, and communities with high student mobility or trauma exposure.

A school leader may value professional inquiry and collaborative learning but face persistent shortages of staff, chronic instability in leadership roles, or mandated reporting loads that leave little time for reflection. In these contexts, the intent to build capital may exist, but the enabling conditions are structurally absent. Schools may find themselves locked in reactive cycles – patching rosters, meeting deadlines – rather than creating space for sustained learning.

Policy frameworks often underestimate these realities. They may prescribe improvement tools without resourcing the time or trust required to use them meaningfully. As Lamb et al. (2014) and others have noted, equity funding alone cannot resolve these issues unless paired with autonomy, flexibility, and long-term support. Schools need more than inputs – they need conditions that protect the relational and intellectual work of improvement.

Without this acknowledgment, the concept of school capital risks sounding aspirational rather than practical – especially to those working in under-resourced environments. Naming the system-level barriers doesn't weaken the argument for school capital; it strengthens it. It reminds us that leadership matters, but so too does policy. Building school capital is both a local and a systemic responsibility.

Yet despite these constraints, the potential of school capital lies in how its dimensions interact. Even in challenging settings, when leaders and communities find ways to strengthen one form of capital, the positive effects can cascade into others. A single investment in coaching or structured collaboration can slowly rebuild trust, deepen professional learning, and improve organisational coherence. Over time, these small but deliberate acts can shift a school's trajectory – not because disadvantage has been eliminated, but because capital is being consciously cultivated.

Intersections and multipliers: when capital works together

Each form of school capital – intellectual, social, organisational, and financial – has value in its own right. But the real power of school capital lies not in these categories alone, but in how they interact. When the forms of capital are activated together, they act as multipliers: amplifying the impact of each other and creating the conditions for sustained, system-level improvement.

This synergy was a key insight in the work of Caldwell and Harris (2008), who emphasised that successful schools do not simply possess more capital – they align and integrate it. A school may have rich intellectual capital in the form of expert teachers, but without social capital – trust, collaboration, shared goals – those insights stay locked in individual classrooms. Similarly, a school may receive additional financial support, but if it lacks the organisational routines to deploy those funds strategically, the impact will be limited.

The interplay between capital types is vividly illustrated in schools that manage to transform not just individual practice but collective culture. One regional primary school, previously low-performing and struggling with disengagement, took deliberate steps to activate all four capitals in concert. First, they invested in intellectual capital by appointing a lead literacy coach from within the team. Then, they built social capital by introducing peer-led instructional rounds. These were scaffolded by simple but consistent organisational routines: protected time for planning, shared inquiry protocols, and short reflection journals. Modest financial resources were used flexibly to release staff for collaboration and to engage a local university partner.

Within three years, both staff morale and student learning had dramatically improved – not because of one program, but because the underlying capital had been woven together with intent.

The School Improvement Tree metaphor makes this visible. Capital is the trunk – the structure through which nutrients flow, supporting the visible outcomes in the canopy. But just like a tree, the strength of the trunk depends on its internal cohesion. When school capital is aligned – when teachers learn together, when trust runs deep, when routines support rather than constrain, and when resources are mobilised with care – the whole school ecosystem becomes more adaptive, more resilient, and more able to grow.

This intersectional view of capital also explains why isolated reform efforts often fall short. A new curriculum, no matter how well-designed, will falter in a school with high staff turnover and low relational trust. A leadership initiative may flounder if teachers lack the time or confidence to implement changes. Conversely, even modest interventions can succeed when they are nested within a rich capital environment.

This also has implications for policy and system support. If systems want to scale improvement, they must do more than deliver toolkits and mandates – they must invest in helping schools build and align their capital. This means funding time for collaboration, supporting distributed leadership, strengthening networks of professional trust, and recognising that improvement is ecological, not mechanical.

It also means shifting the improvement question from 'What's the right program?' to 'What's the current health of our school capital?' This reframing moves the focus from technical implementation to cultural and structural readiness. It encourages school leaders and system designers alike to consider how different forms of capital can be cultivated deliberately – and how alignment, not uniformity, is the key to sustainability.

In short, capital works best when it works together. It is not just a set of assets, but a dynamic system. And when that system is nurtured, the possibilities for learning – and for meaningful, lasting change – expand dramatically.

Building and investing in what matters most

Ultimately, building school capital is a deliberate act of leadership and learning. It is not about chasing novelty, but about strengthening the conditions that allow schools – and those within them – to thrive.

School improvement is too often pursued as a matter of policy direction or program design, when in fact its success hinges on something deeper: the internal capacity of schools to learn, adapt, and grow. This chapter has argued that such capacity is not accidental – it is built, and it is built through school capital.

Across the four dimensions – intellectual, social, organisational, and financial – we see that capital is not just about what schools have, but how they use it. It is not a checklist of resources or a measure of affluence. It is the infrastructure of learning. Strong capital enables schools to act with coherence, compassion, and creativity. Weak or misaligned capital leaves even the best strategies vulnerable to collapse under the weight of daily demands.

What matters most, then, is not the pursuit of novelty, but the stewardship of what **already exists**. The most powerful resources for improvement are often already within schools – if we choose to see and nurture them. Teachers' insights, team relationships, school routines, funding flexibility – these are not background features of reform. They are the reform.

You just have to look; it's always been here. When schools are intentional about cultivating and aligning these elements, they shift the very conditions under which all learning takes place. And at the heart of that stewardship lies curiosity – the willingness to see familiar resources with fresh eyes and ask how they might serve learning in new ways.

And this has moral significance. Because capital is not evenly distributed, investing in it is also an act of equity. Schools serving disadvantaged communities must be supported to build their capital deliberately and sustainably – not just through funding, but through trust, time, and partnership. My research and experience affirm that moral purpose, curiosity, and capital together form the bedrock of long-term, system-wide improvement. But without capital, the other two cannot fully take root.

This is not easy work. It takes time to build trust, to embed routines, to share knowledge, and to allocate resources wisely. It also takes courage – to resist quick fixes, to hold space for learning, and to honour the complexity of school life. But it is in this complexity that the most meaningful change happens.

From insight to action: school capital – the conditions for growth

School capital doesn't grow by accident – it grows through intention, reflection, and shared effort. These prompts invite teachers, leaders, and system partners to consider where their next step might begin.

For teachers:

- How often do we make time to share what we're learning with each other?
- Are there informal networks or 'knowledge bridges' within the school – and how could we strengthen them?
- Where do I feel intellectually stretched, socially connected, and supported to try something new?

For principals:

- Which dimension of capital – intellectual, social, organisational, or financial – needs the most attention in our school right now?
- Are we building trust through transparency, dialogue, and shared learning?
- Do our structures (for example, meeting formats, timetables, resource allocations) enable growth, or constrain it?

For systems:

- Are we investing in long-term capability or short-term output?
- How do we assess whether schools are thriving – not just surviving?
- Do we create the conditions for networked learning, shared inquiry, and the respectful exchange of expertise?

Building school capital is not a project with an end point – it is a continuous act of stewardship. When curiosity and moral purpose are threaded through this capital, schools gain the capacity not only to improve but to keep growing from within.

And the Curious Cat?

In this chapter, it lingers not in the library or the classroom, but behind the staffroom door and beside the whiteboard in the leadership office. It prowls the places where decisions are made, wondering whether time will be protected, voices will be heard, and learning will be allowed to unfold. It knows that capital cannot be forced – but it can be fostered. And when it is, the ground beneath reform becomes firmer, more fertile, and far more likely to grow something that lasts.

Afterword: strengthening the trunk

Improvement that lasts doesn't just rely on great ideas – it depends on the strength of what holds them up. School capital is that strength. It's the trunk of the tree: steady, alive, often unnoticed. It supports every branch of reform and every leaf of innovation. And like any trunk, it grows slowly, layer by layer, through seasons of challenge and change.

This chapter has made the case that schools don't just need vision or strategy – they need the internal conditions that make those things possible. When capital is nurtured deliberately and in alignment, the work of teaching becomes more collaborative, more sustainable, and more human. The school becomes not just a workplace but a place of shared purpose and ongoing learning.

As we move into Chapter 5 on reawakening inquiry, the focus shifts from the conditions to the practices that bring curiosity back to life. But it is the capital we've explored here – intellectual, social, organisational, and financial – that gives those practices room to breathe.

In the end, deep school capital isn't something we import. It's something we notice, nurture, and grow – layer by layer, conversation by conversation. The strength we seek is already in the room, already in the relationships, already in the routines. *You just have to look. It's always been here.*

The Curious Cat, tail flicking, doesn't chase the next shiny idea. It stays with the slow work. It knows that deep roots make tall trees. And it knows, too, that strong trunks don't just appear – they are grown, together.

CHAPTER 5
Reawakening Inquiry – Practices That Bring Curiosity to Life

BIG IDEAS IN THIS CHAPTER

Curiosity is not a bonus – it's a vital part of effective teaching and learning. But in many schools it lies dormant beneath routines, mandates, and standardisation.

Reawakening inquiry means changing habits, not just structures. It calls for brave reflection and a willingness to disrupt the comfort of 'how we've always done it'.

Curiosity lives in questions, not answers. Teaching practices that value deep thinking, exploration, and student voice are central to its revival.

Culture matters. When leaders model curiosity and protect time for reflection, schools create the conditions for professional and pedagogical inquiry to flourish.

This chapter asks:

- How do we bring curiosity back to life in real classrooms?
- What shifts in practice, culture, and leadership will sustain it?

> *'Tell me, what is it you plan to do with your one wild and precious life?'* – Mary Oliver

A sleeping giant

In many schools, curiosity lies dormant – not extinguished, but subdued by the routines of compliance, the weight of accountability, and the momentum of tradition. It lives just beneath the surface of worksheets, program guides, and timetables. Occasionally, it stirs: in a classroom debate that veers off script, in a student's unexpected question, in a teacher's quiet experiment with a new approach. But too often, the structures and cultures of schooling smother the spark before it catches flame.

This suppression is rarely deliberate. It stems from high-stakes testing, the over-prescription of curricula, and a policy narrative that too often prioritises visible outcomes at the expense of authentic engagement. When the curriculum is narrowed to maximise test scores, when timetables crowd out space for exploration, when the energy of a school becomes focused on audit rather than inquiry, curiosity is the first casualty. Time-strapped, accountability-driven teachers can easily become trapped into delivering rather than co-creating, managing rather than inspiring.

And yet curiosity is the starting point for learning. It draws us toward what we do not yet know. It invites us to dwell in uncertainty with openness rather than fear. Children are born curious, driven by an intrinsic desire to explore – a point Susan Engel (2011) underscores. But as formal education progresses, that natural inquisitiveness is too often narrowed by standardised expectations and prescriptive pedagogies. International studies such as PISA have shown that countries with highly standardised assessment regimes often experience a steady decline in student motivation and engagement over time (OECD, 2019b). The link between accountability pressure and the suppression of curiosity is troubling – and increasingly clear.

This chapter explores what it takes to reawaken inquiry – not as a pedagogical technique alone, but as a cultural shift. It examines how curiosity can be cultivated deliberately across three domains: classroom practice, professional learning, and leadership. It argues that reawakening inquiry is not about adding something new, but about remembering something essential. And it builds on the earlier chapters: moral purpose gives us the ethical foundation; school capital provides the enabling conditions.

Together, they create the space in which curiosity is not merely permitted, but prioritised.

When educators teach with curiosity, lead with inquiry, and create space for wonder, they don't just improve learning – they transform it. They build environments where students and teachers alike are invited to be thinkers, explorers, co-creators. Reawakening inquiry, then, is not a task for a single classroom or a single moment. It is a long, deliberate, hopeful process. And it begins wherever someone chooses to ask a better question.

Classroom cultures of inquiry

In classrooms where curiosity flourishes, the dominant rhythm is not delivery but discovery. Learning begins not with answers but with questions – open, provocative, sometimes unanswerable. These are classrooms where students are expected to wonder, puzzle, make connections, and speak their thinking aloud (Ritchhart et al., 2011). The teacher becomes not a transmitter of knowledge, but a co-learner and facilitator, structuring the environment to nurture dialogue, perspective-taking, and intellectual risk-taking.

Such classrooms are structured for exploration. They include visible thinking routines, flexible groupings, space for sustained dialogue. They protect time for reflection. They embed metacognition, inviting students to consider not just what they know but how they came to know it. Teachers in these spaces frame lessons with questions rather than objectives. They model uncertainty. They celebrate productive struggle (Claxton, 2008).

Consider a Year 8 humanities unit on migration. The inquiry question was deceptively simple: 'What makes a place feel like home?' Students explored family stories, immigration records, cultural artefacts. They constructed understanding through research, discussion, and empathy interviews. The culmination was a student-led exhibition showcasing diverse definitions of belonging, shaped by lived experience rather than textbook summaries. One parent, after visiting her child's project showcase, said: 'It's the first time I've seen him take the lead in learning. He wasn't just reciting facts – he was telling stories, asking questions, explaining his thinking.' These moments signal something deeper than academic success: a transformation in how young people see themselves as learners.

What distinguishes such classrooms is that knowledge is in motion – not fixed and inert, but co-constructed and evolving. Students are not passive consumers; they are active theorists, critics, creators. Dialogic teaching, as explored by Alexander (2008), provides a powerful frame here: using talk not only to share ideas but to think together, challenge assumptions, and stretch reasoning.

In one Year 9 science class, students worked in teams to design and test hypotheses about energy efficiency in the school building. Rather than follow a pre-set worksheet, they negotiated variables, revised approaches, and presented findings to community engineers. The result was not only deeper understanding but a sense of ownership over learning.

Assessment looks different too. It values depth over speed, process over performance. Feedback focuses on insight, not just correctness. Students are not passive recipients of evaluation but participants in a co-construction of knowledge (Kashdan, 2009). In one upper primary classroom, students curated weekly 'wonder reflections', including annotated diagrams, voice recordings, peer feedback – building a rich tapestry of evidence far beyond traditional tests.

But none of this happens unless classrooms are emotionally safe. Curiosity flourishes when students feel secure enough to take risks (Engel, 2011). In high-pressure environments dominated by testing, that safety erodes – and with it, students' willingness to ask questions. In contrast, classrooms where questioning is welcomed and ambiguity is embraced become spaces where deep learning can unfold.

Such classrooms are not chaotic. They are purposeful. But their purpose is expansive: to help students become not only more knowledgeable but more curious, thoughtful, self-directed. This shift begins when a teacher asks, 'What do you notice?' instead of 'Who knows the answer?' And it builds, slowly, through routines that honour thoughtfulness, spaces that make learning visible, and relationships that centre dignity.

But if students are to experience this, teachers must be immersed in curiosity-rich professional learning themselves.

Professional learning that sparks curiosity

Curiosity is contagious – but only if adults experience it. Too often, professional learning mirrors the very practices schools seek to avoid in classrooms: passive presentations, generic strategies, little room for dialogue. Teachers are treated as technicians to be retrained, not as thinkers engaged in the craft of teaching. This models the very compliance-driven culture that stifles curiosity.

But when professional learning is inquiry-driven, everything shifts. Teachers come alive when invited to explore their own questions. Peer coaching, action research, collaborative inquiry teams – these create the conditions for shared exploration. Teachers who are trusted to pose problems, gather data, test approaches, reflect openly, build not only knowledge but professional confidence (Timperley et al., 2007).

Curious professional learning is rooted in relevance. It emerges from the realities of the classroom, not from abstractions. It gives teachers permission to ask: 'Why does this strategy engage some learners but not others? What assumptions underpin our expectations? What might we try differently?' In curious schools, professional learning is not a calendar item – it is a culture.

One school built a 'Learning Lab' model where staff volunteered to open classrooms to colleagues for observation and feedback – not for evaluation, but for mutual inquiry. Teachers posed wondering questions – 'What do you notice about how students engage?' – and reflected together. Over time, trust deepened, and professional curiosity became embedded. A Year 2 teacher observed: 'The most powerful moment wasn't when I got answers – it was when someone helped me ask a better question.'

Crucially, this kind of learning supports teacher engagement and renewal. Curious teachers are more likely to stay. They report greater job satisfaction, stronger professional identity, deeper collegial trust. In high-pressure environments, curiosity becomes a buffer against burnout – and a driver of innovation. Curious schools become more resilient, more adaptive. And that resilience matters most when complexity, disruption, or challenge arrive.

Ultimately, professional learning that sparks curiosity does more than improve practice. It restores purpose. It reminds educators that they are engaged in a deeply human, deeply hopeful endeavour. In doing so, it connects directly to the argument that curiosity, moral purpose, and capital must work in concert if school improvement is to be both effective and sustainable.

Leadership that protects and provokes

Reawakening inquiry also requires leadership that does more than manage. Curious leaders do not dictate – they create the conditions for exploration.

They lead with questions. They model reflection. They hold space for dialogue and change.

This leadership is both stance and structure. Curious leaders ask: 'What are we noticing? What are we learning from our students? Where are we stuck? Where are we thriving?' They resist the pressure to appear all-knowing and instead model vulnerability, reflection, wonder.

At the same time, they build routines: inquiry protocols, collaborative planning cycles, peer observation, feedback. Without such structures, inquiry fades. Curious leadership is not laissez-faire – it is deliberate, rhythmical, intentional.

Perhaps most importantly, curious leadership is values-driven. It links curiosity to moral purpose. It asks not only 'How can we improve?' but 'How can we do right by all our students?' Inquiry becomes a tool for equity – a pathway to justice.

Curious leadership also means navigating tension. It challenges performative habits – over-reliance on narrow data, fear of experimentation, cultures of perfectionism. It reframes failure as learning. It embraces the uncomfortable questions as doorways to deeper insight.

And curious leaders are networked learners. They look beyond their own walls. They build partnerships, engage with research, join coalitions. They lead with humility. They listen.

Ultimately, they build cultures where asking questions is not risky, where uncertainty is not weakness, where learning is not reserved for students alone. In such places, culture shifts. Innovation becomes continuous. Leadership becomes a shared, hopeful act.

From spark to system: weaving curiosity into school culture

Reawakening inquiry is not a short-term intervention. It is a long game. It requires cultural commitment and the willingness to challenge routines that no longer serve learning. It asks schools to be more than delivery systems. It asks them to be communities of learners.

When curiosity is reawakened, effects ripple. Students ask better questions. Teachers collaborate more deeply. Leaders listen more intently. Parents become partners. Improvement ceases to be something done *to* people – it becomes something grown *with* them.

Yet this is not easy work. It means confronting inertia – not only in systems and structures, but in ourselves. It means noticing defaults, questioning the comfortable, choosing to be curious even when it's inconvenient. It requires courage – not individual bravery alone, but collective resolve.

Fortunately, sparks of curiosity already exist in every school. The task is to notice them, protect them, fan them into flame. This is the work of culture, not compliance – of relationship, not routine. It is also the work of hope.

Inquiry invites us to believe that things can be different – that learning can be deeper, that schools can become more human, more just, more alive. Curiosity is not merely a technique. It is an ethic. A stance. A way of being.

When embedded across classrooms, staffrooms, systems, it becomes a force for lasting change.

From insight to action: practices that bring curiosity to life

Reawakening inquiry starts small – in the questions we ask, the spaces we create, and the trust we build. These practical moves can help translate the ideas in this chapter into everyday action – in classrooms, across teams, and through leadership at every level.

For teachers:

- Invite genuine student questions into the heart of lessons – not as a warm-up, but as a driver of learning.
- Shift from task-driven planning to question-driven planning: 'What do I want students to wonder about?'
- Model curiosity openly – share when you don't know, think aloud, and celebrate moments of shared discovery.

For principals:

- Protect space for teacher inquiry (not just instructional delivery): timetable collaborative inquiry cycles into the professional learning calendar.
- Reframe staff meetings as opportunities to explore shared questions of practice – not just operational updates.
- Recognise and affirm pedagogical risk-taking; make curiosity safe and valued.

For systems:

- Incentivise inquiry-rich professional learning – not compliance-driven PD.
- Support networks of schools experimenting with curiosity-driven approaches and share the learning.
- Shift performance narratives: broaden success metrics to include evidence of engagement, exploration, and deep learning – not just test outcomes.

Each small step toward curiosity strengthens the culture that sustains it. Choose one action to start – and watch where the questions lead.

The Curious Cat watches all this unfold. Not with urgency, but with patience. It knows that curiosity cannot be forced – but it can be invited. It can be protected. And it can, when conditions are right, come roaring back to life.

Afterword: turning inquiry into momentum

The reawakening of inquiry begins with a mindset – but it must grow through action. This chapter has shown that, while often treated as a peripheral quality, curiosity may in fact be one of the most underappreciated drivers of meaningful learning and adaptive leadership – especially when harnessed with intention and care.

But knowing that isn't enough. The challenge now is to build the structures, habits, and relationships that let curiosity thrive every day.

Start small: Begin a meeting with a genuine question. Give students space to shape the direction of a lesson. Invite a colleague to co-reflect on a challenge rather than seeking a quick fix. These practices might seem modest, but they create momentum. Over time, they change culture.

Schools don't transform through programs alone – they shift when the people inside them begin to see differently, ask differently, and lead differently. The work is ongoing, but it is deeply human and deeply hopeful.

Curiosity, once stirred, can spread. And once it spreads, it can stick.

The Curious Cat would be the first to remind us: the real work of change doesn't begin at the finish line – it begins with a single step, taken with purpose, and a willingness to see where the question might lead.

INTERLUDE

Before the Shadow Falls

'Two roads diverged in a yellow wood …' – Robert Frost

There is always a moment – quiet, unannounced – when a choice is made. Sometimes by a teacher in the middle of a lesson, sometimes by a leadership team behind closed doors, sometimes by a system deciding what matters most. It is the moment when the path of school improvement splits.

One path is familiar. It is the path of plans and protocols, performance charts and strategic frameworks. It promises order, accountability, and incremental growth. It moves quickly, efficiently, and often feels like progress. But it can become narrow. In its speed and simplicity, it sometimes misses the deeper currents beneath the surface – the fears, the tensions, the inequalities that shape learning long before a child steps into the classroom.

The other path is more difficult to follow. It does not begin with answers but with questions. It resists prescription in favour of reflection. It asks not only *how* we are improving, but *why*, and *for whom*. This path meanders. It pauses. It notices what has been overlooked and listens longer than expected. It makes room for discomfort and welcomes complexity, not as a threat but as a teacher.

The School Improvement Tree – first glimpsed earlier and explored in full in the next chapter –offers a living metaphor for the deeper path of change. Its roots run deep in moral purpose, as laid down in Chapter 3 – the ethical why that anchors the work. Its trunk is formed by school capital developed in Chapter 4 – conditions that give the school strength, coherence, and the capacity to grow from within. And its canopy, based on understandings of curiosity developed in Chapter 5 and stretching toward possibility, shelters more than just achievement. It offers space for belonging, creativity, and trust – the very qualities that make learning meaningful and reform sustainable.

The Cat lingers here, too. Tail flicking. Eyes wide. It follows not the obvious route but the overlooked one. It finds meaning in the shadows and movement at the margins. Because that is where change so often begins – not with clarity, but with curiosity.

Not in the spotlight, but just before the shadow falls.

CHAPTER 6
The School Improvement Tree – Growth from the Inside Out

> **BIG IDEAS IN THIS CHAPTER**
>
> School improvement is not a formula – it's a living process. The Tree metaphor helps us see how growth happens when moral purpose, school capital, and curiosity are all present and aligned.
>
> Roots, trunk, and canopy each play a role. Moral purpose anchors the work, school capital enables it, and curiosity animates it – driving engagement, creativity, and resilience.
>
> Improvement is relational, layered, and non-linear. It takes time, care, and coherence – not just more programs or tighter accountability.
>
> Curiosity flourishes when schools grow from the inside out. Cultures of trust, collective learning, and shared purpose create the conditions for sustained change.
>
> This chapter asks:
>
> - What part of the Tree needs nourishment in your school?
> - How might your roots, trunk, and canopy better support meaningful learning?

'What the roots drink, the leaves whisper.' – Rumi

The School Improvement Tree

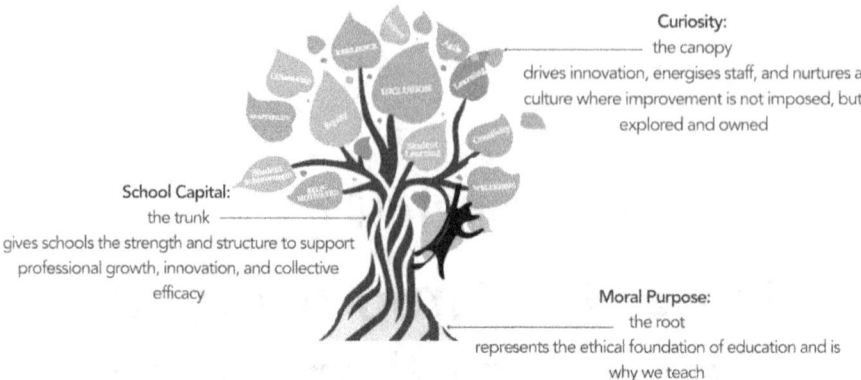

A living metaphor for sustainable change

School improvement often suffers from short-term thinking. Initiatives are launched with urgency, implemented under pressure, and evaluated too quickly. The result is fragmentation – flashes of progress that rarely take hold. What's needed instead is a model that understands growth as organic, relational, and long-term.

The School Improvement Tree offers such a model. It is not a checklist or a framework. It is a living metaphor – one that reflects how deep, lasting improvement actually works. In this metaphor, the roots represent moral purpose, the ethical foundation of a school's work. The trunk symbolises school capital – the strength and structure that enables growth. And the canopy embodies curiosity and its outcomes – the visible flourishing of ideas, inquiry, agency, and engagement.

The Tree grows from the inside out. Its strength lies not in what is imposed from above, but in what is cultivated within.

But as with any tree, what matters most is not what we see above the ground, but what lies beneath. Before we can talk about visible growth, we must begin with the roots – with the moral purpose that gives school improvement both its meaning and its strength.

Rooted in action: enacting moral purpose in school life

Every tree begins underground. Its root system is unseen, yet it determines everything that follows – drawing nutrients, anchoring the trunk, and sustaining growth through drought and storm. In schools, moral purpose plays the same role. It provides stability, meaning, and direction. Without deep roots, the system is vulnerable to superficial reform, quick fixes, and cultural drift. With them, it can grow, stretch, and weather adversity.

Michael Fullan (2011) defines moral purpose as the commitment to 'raising the bar and closing the gap for all students'. It is an ethical stance, not just a strategic one. In the most effective schools, this is not a slogan or a paragraph on a strategic plan – it is a living commitment that shapes how the school operates. It informs who is listened to, what is resourced, and how time is used. When difficult decisions arise – as they always do – it is moral purpose that provides the compass.

You can see moral purpose in action in how a school handles conflict. Is the response to behavioural challenges framed by empathy or control? Are difficult staff conversations deferred, or are they approached with clarity and compassion because students deserve better? Moral purpose also lives in data conversations – where the focus is not only on gaps, but on the children behind the numbers. It lives in timetables that prioritise literacy and numeracy without compromising curiosity, in recruitment processes that seek shared values, and in school rituals that centre inclusion and respect.

Hargreaves and Fullan (2012) argue that 'the deepest and most sustainable change comes from the inside out', rooted in a profound sense of responsibility for the lives of students and communities. That responsibility must extend beyond the classroom – it must inform how schools interact with their communities, how they respond to systemic inequality, and how they use their influence to advocate for more-just conditions. Moral purpose is what compels a school to ask: 'Are we serving all learners? Are we lifting those furthest behind? Are we creating a future that is worthy of our students' potential?'

Schools with strong roots don't panic with every shift in government policy or funding formula. They know who they are. They don't chase every initiative, nor do they reject change reflexively. Instead, they engage with new ideas from a place of grounded identity. They adapt selectively – anchored by clarity of mission and values. Conversely, when moral purpose is weak or unclear, schools can become chameleons – constantly reacting, mimicking trends, and mistaking activity for impact. They may appear busy or even successful on the surface, but underneath, the culture is brittle. Their growth is cosmetic, not cultural.

Leaders play a pivotal role in cultivating and protecting moral purpose. This involves more than inspirational messaging. It requires deliberate structures for collective reflection, honest dialogue about trade-offs, and consistent decision-making that aligns with professed values. As Campbell (2003) notes, 'ethics in education leadership is not about grand gestures – it is about small, repeated actions that honour the dignity of each person in the community'. Leaders must model moral purpose in how they listen, how they allocate time and resources, and how they respond when mistakes are made.

This might look like a leadership team that invites diverse voices into decision-making – not just for consultation, but for co-construction. It might involve rethinking staff meetings to include time for reflecting on student voice or revisiting the school's mission in light of new challenges. It could mean pausing a major initiative if it begins to drift from purpose, even if it looks good on a spreadsheet. Schools that are serious about moral purpose build it into their routines: they assess not only what they are doing, but why they are doing it – and for whom.

Teachers, too, must be part of this work. Moral purpose cannot rest solely with senior leaders. It must be woven into the professional identity of all staff. This means creating safe spaces for teachers to talk openly about what matters in their practice, to examine bias, to share dilemmas, and to support one another in pursuing equity. Professional learning should not only focus on curriculum or pedagogy – it should also attend to purpose, agency, and ethical reflection (Timperley, 2011).

Yet even the strongest roots must be fed and renewed. And in the rich soil of schools, moral purpose is never simple or uncontested. It must be named, examined, and contextualised – not imposed as a single truth. That is where the next layer of growth begins.

Rooted in meaning: contesting and contextualising moral purpose

Every strong tree draws its strength from the soil. In the case of school improvement, that soil is moral purpose. It is what anchors a school's actions in meaning, beyond metrics, programs, or reform fads. But while moral purpose is widely invoked in education – as a compass, a driver, a source of integrity – it is not a neutral or universally agreed idea. It is shaped by history, community values, cultural context, and lived experience. For some, it emerges from social justice or faith traditions. For others, it's expressed through public service, intergenerational responsibility, or the belief in every child's right to thrive. Its power lies in its depth, but so does its complexity.

Too often, moral purpose is presented as if it were singular or obvious – when in fact, it can be a site of tension. What is 'right' for one community may feel misguided or even harmful to another. One school's definition of success might prioritise academic excellence; another might emphasise wellbeing, cultural identity, or civic contribution. A principal's moral stance on attendance might clash with the realities of a family struggling with housing instability. Teachers might disagree on how best to serve students with learning difficulties – some advocating for integration, others for specialist settings. These differences are not just logistical; they reflect competing visions of what education is for.

Recognising the contested nature of moral purpose doesn't weaken it – it strengthens it. It invites dialogue. It demands reflection. It urges schools and systems not to adopt pre-packaged values but to surface, negotiate, and live out their purpose in relationship with others. In this way, moral purpose becomes both ethical and epistemological: not only a set of commitments, but a way of seeking truth through engagement.

Schools that build from moral purpose don't avoid hard questions – they walk toward them. They name what matters, even when it's uncomfortable. They hold themselves accountable, not only to benchmarks but to children's dignity and to their communities' trust. And they return, again and again, to the why beneath the what. This is what roots them. It gives them the moral clarity to resist harmful pressures and the flexibility to adapt while staying true to their core.

At its best, moral purpose is not imposed – it's grown. In one remote Aboriginal community school, the leadership team worked with Elders to co-develop a moral vision for learning grounded in cultural continuity and youth empowerment. In a large multicultural secondary school, moral purpose became the cornerstone for transforming teacher appraisal – not as compliance, but as a collective inquiry into how well staff were serving their most vulnerable students. These examples show how moral purpose, when alive and locally grounded, can be a force not only for improvement but for transformation.

The roots of school improvement, then, are not abstract. They live in conversations, histories, convictions, and relationships. When educators are clear about what they stand for – and when they are willing to keep asking what that means in practice – they create the kind of moral foundation that can sustain the weight of real, enduring change.

But recognising the complexity of moral purpose is only the start. To sustain it through the inevitable pressures of daily school life requires deliberate cultivation – the ongoing work of aligning words and actions, even when conditions are less than ideal.

Cultivating the soil: sustaining moral purpose over time

Moral purpose does not simply appear in schools; it must be cultivated. Like healthy soil, it requires attention, renewal, and care – especially when conditions are harsh. In education systems shaped by policy churn, high-stakes accountability, and increasing complexity, moral purpose can be quietly eroded. Even the most values-driven schools can drift toward expedience when resources are stretched or performance pressures mount.

This erosion is rarely sudden. It happens incrementally: when conversations focus more on compliance than on learning; when difficult truths are avoided for the sake of comfort or cohesion; when staff wellbeing is sacrificed to meet short-term targets. Over time, the shared 'why' begins to fade, replaced by a culture of busyness that mimics improvement but lacks deep intent.

Sustaining moral purpose, then, is not a passive act – it is deliberate, disciplined work. It involves building routines of ethical reflection, holding space for complexity, and protecting time for dialogue. It requires leaders to resist the allure of quick wins when they come at the cost of integrity, and to model vulnerability when certainty is elusive.

This is where the idea of rhythm becomes critical. As David Hopkins and Wayne Craig (2016) have noted, every school beats to two rhythms: the rhythm of the school year – marked by term calendars, deadlines, and system cycles – and the rhythm of development, which unfolds more slowly through trust, reflection, and cultural growth. When these rhythms fall out of sync, schools may appear productive but lose their moral centre. But when leaders align them – when the cadence of daily work supports, rather than undermines, deeper purpose – schools become more than responsive; they become resilient.

Cultivating the soil of moral purpose also involves embracing collective authorship. Moral clarity does not come from one person at the top – it is shaped and reshaped through shared inquiry. Staff need structured opportunities to reflect on their practice, challenge assumptions, and reconnect with what brought them to the work. Students, families, and communities must also be part of this conversation – not simply as recipients of moral purpose, but as co-creators of it.

This ongoing cultivation also demands courage – the courage to speak up when practices drift from purpose, to confront injustices that systems may normalise, and to say no to initiatives that look good on paper but misalign with the needs of children. It requires staying grounded in complexity without becoming cynical, and hopeful without becoming naïve.

Like all living things, moral purpose grows best in healthy conditions – but it can also take root in difficult soil. Some of the most powerful examples of purpose-driven practice come from schools in challenging contexts, where educators resist deficit narratives and build cultures of care, belonging, and excellence. What these schools share is not perfection, but persistence. They return again and again to the foundational questions: 'Who are we here for? What do we believe about young people? What kind of future are we preparing them for?'

When these questions are asked not once but routinely – at staff meetings, in appraisal conversations, during curriculum design, and in crisis – then moral purpose moves from abstraction to action. It becomes not only the root of improvement, but the soil in which transformation can take hold.

Purpose alone is not enough. For schools to translate moral clarity into action – to turn aspiration into impact – they need strength and structure. This is the work of school capital, the trunk that allows schools to stand tall and support lasting growth.

School capital as the trunk: building capacity for growth

If the root system gives life, the trunk gives strength. In the School Improvement Tree, the trunk represents school capital – a concept developed by Caldwell and Harris (2008) to describe the accumulated resources and capacities that enable a school to turn intent into action. It is this structural core that allows purpose to be realised, inquiry to be sustained, and innovation to be scaled. Without a strong trunk, even the most compelling moral purpose or imaginative canopy will falter.

School capital is multidimensional and deeply relational. It comprises four interdependent domains:

- **Intellectual capital** is the collective professional knowledge and expertise of staff. It includes subject knowledge, instructional skill, and assessment literacy, but it also encompasses the ability to reflect, question, and adapt in the face of complexity. Schools with rich intellectual capital cultivate a culture of learning among teachers, not just students.
- **Social capital** refers to the quality of relationships and trust within the school community. It is built through collaboration, shared responsibility, and respectful dialogue (Bryk & Schneider, 2002). When social capital is high, staff are more likely to take risks, offer feedback, and engage in joint problem-solving. When it is low, silos form, resistance grows, and even the best ideas struggle to spread.
- **Organisational capital** describes the systems, structures, and routines that embed effective practice and enable scalability. These include team meeting protocols, instructional coaching frameworks, school-wide planning cycles, and internal communication mechanisms (Harris, 2010). Organisational capital does not guarantee learning, but it prevents good practice from being accidental or idiosyncratic.
- **Financial capital** includes the material resources – funding, staffing, facilities, and technology – that make professional learning, equity interventions, and innovation possible. While money alone does not create improvement, it enables responsiveness and reduces the strain that can lead to reactive or compliance-driven cultures. Targeted financial capital, aligned with learning priorities, amplifies other forms of capital (Darling-Hammond, 2010).

What makes the concept of school capital so powerful is its interdependence. Caldwell and Harris (2008) emphasise that the four domains do not operate in isolation. Intellectual capital, for instance, is strengthened by high levels of social capital – trust enables the sharing of knowledge. Organisational capital supports the embedding of intellectual practices into school routines. Financial capital, when used strategically, enables time for reflection, resources for professional learning, and investment in leadership growth. Schools that improve sustainably are those that attend to this balance.

In contrast, over-reliance on a single form of capital creates distortion. A school may, for example, purchase state-of-the-art technology (financial capital) but fail to develop staff capacity to use it well (intellectual capital) or provide time for shared learning (organisational capital). Another school may invest in leadership structures (organisational capital) without cultivating the relationships that make those structures meaningful (social capital). The result is fragility disguised as progress.

Building the trunk takes time. It is a cumulative process of deliberate learning, investment, and trust-building. Unlike quick-win interventions, capital growth requires sustained focus and distributed effort. It depends not only on leadership vision, but on broad-based engagement.

Leaders play a crucial role in diagnosing and developing school capital. One useful starting point is to conduct a capital health check – a reflection across the four domains. Which areas are strongest? Which are neglected? What connections are missing? These conversations help surface hidden strengths and gaps in the school's capacity for growth.

Practical strategies to strengthen the trunk include:

- **Investing in professional learning** that is job-embedded, inquiry-based, and aligned with school values
- **Creating cross-role teams** that draw on diverse expertise and encourage collective responsibility
- **Establishing shared routines** – like data discussion protocols or co-planning templates – that make collaborative practice visible and repeatable
- **Providing time for reflection**, not just implementation, so that staff can consolidate, adapt, and improve over time
- **Targeting resources** toward areas that build long-term capacity rather than short-term compliance.

In schools with strong trunks, leadership is distributed and developmental. Authority is not concentrated in a single person or position, but woven through the culture. Leaders at all levels see themselves as stewards of capital – supporting others to grow, connect, and lead. Teachers are not just implementers of change – they are co-creators of it.

This form of leadership requires a shift from control to enablement. It involves listening as much as directing, asking as much as answering. It means creating the conditions where professional capital can flourish – not by mandating collaboration, but by nurturing the trust, time, and tools that make it possible.

Importantly, the growth of school capital is not an internal matter alone. Systems must play their part. When external policy demands crowd out reflection, when funding is inconsistent or inequitable, when reform cycles are short and superficial – capital is depleted. Conversely, when systems invest in trust-building, support schools to collaborate, and protect space for leadership learning, capital accumulates.

A strong trunk does more than support existing structures – it enables upward and outward growth. It allows a school to stretch toward curiosity, innovation, and student agency without falling apart. It holds steady when the environment is uncertain, when leaders change, or when pressures mount. And it makes the canopy of learning not just possible, but sustainable.

And yet no tree grows for itself alone. The visible life of a school – the engagement of students, the creativity of teachers, the vitality of learning – is expressed through its canopy. This is where curiosity breathes life into improvement and makes learning joyful, visible, and sustainable.

Curiosity and its outcomes as the canopy

At the top of the Tree lies the canopy – the visible expression of the school's inner life. It is what you notice first: the learning, the energy, the questions in the air. In this metaphor, the canopy represents curiosity and its outcomes – the flourishing of inquiry, agency, creativity, and deep learning.

Curiosity is not a luxury in education. It is a condition for growth. It is both a psychological disposition and a professional discipline. Todd Kashdan et al. (2020) describe curiosity as the drive to explore, learn, and embrace uncertainty. It is the engine behind scientific discovery, artistic insight, and pedagogical innovation. In education, curiosity manifests when teachers wonder aloud about student needs, when students pursue questions beyond the curriculum, and when leaders view problems as opportunities rather than obstacles.

In schools where the canopy is vibrant, curiosity can be seen and felt:

- Students are **engaged**, ask questions, and take intellectual risks.
- Teachers **experiment** with new strategies and reflect on their impact.
- Leadership fosters **dialogue**, not just delivery.
- Innovation arises **from within** – not as compliance with external mandates, but as lived inquiry born from professional autonomy and shared purpose.

These are not decorative traits. They are signs of a healthy, adaptive school culture. As Susan Engel (2011) argues, curiosity 'does not survive in environments that are controlling, punitive, or hurried'. When schools are dominated by fear, micromanagement, or unrelenting performance pressure, curiosity withers. But when conditions support exploration, when relationships are safe, and when learning is public, the canopy thrives.

Crucially, the canopy nourishes the rest of the Tree. Just as trees draw sunlight through their leaves and convert it into energy, schools draw strength from curiosity. It reawakens purpose, fuels professional engagement, and makes learning joyful and sustainable. In high-functioning schools, curiosity is not a distraction from rigour – it is a pathway to it.

This canopy can take many forms. It might look like a Year 5 classroom where students design experiments based on questions they generated themselves. It might be seen in a staff team reflecting on a failed strategy – not to assign blame, but to extract insight. It might show up in a school that invites families to co-create learning experiences, recognising that community voices hold wisdom worth exploring. What matters is not the form but the ethos: curiosity is alive, invited, and patterned.

Yet, curiosity is fragile. It must be protected. In many systems, it is at risk – not from neglect, but from structural conditions that work against it. Time poverty, over-scheduled timetables, punitive accountability regimes, and a narrow definition of success can all choke curiosity before it has a chance to grow (Sahlberg, 2011). Teachers cannot sustain inquiry if every minute is spoken for. Students will not ask bold questions if they believe there is only one right answer. And leaders will not model curiosity if their roles are reduced to compliance and risk minimisation.

To protect the canopy, schools must design for curiosity, not just hope for it. This means building routines and structures that make exploration habitual. For example:

- Embedding **inquiry cycles** into team planning – where teachers identify problems of practice, explore research, test changes, and reflect
- Establishing **cross-role learning groups** – so that staff learn from one another across disciplines and experience levels
- Redesigning **staff meetings** around professional questions rather than operational updates
- Celebrating **process learning**, not just product achievement.

When these practices become part of the rhythm of school life, curiosity shifts from being occasional to being cultural. It becomes not something you make time for, but something you build around.

The canopy also depends on psychological safety – a term popularised by Amy Edmondson (1999) to describe environments where people feel safe to speak up, take risks, and be themselves. In curious schools, mistakes are seen as learning moments, not failures. Questions are treated as contributions, not distractions. Diversity of perspective is welcomed, not flattened. These norms are critical if inquiry is to become a shared practice rather than an individual habit.

Leadership plays a central role in sustaining the canopy. Curious leaders ask before they answer. They model vulnerability by admitting what they don't know. They create forums for dialogue, encourage dissent, and celebrate experimentation. They shift the focus from 'Are we compliant?' to 'What are we learning?' This stance not only supports professional growth but also fosters collective efficacy – the belief that the team can improve together (Bandura, 1997; Donohoo et al., 2016).

Curious leadership also involves active protection of the conditions that allow curiosity to thrive. In systems where time is compressed, performance pressures dominate, or rigid hierarchies persist, curiosity can quickly become marginalised. Wise leaders recognise this risk and act deliberately to shield inquiry-rich spaces from erosion. They create schedules that prioritise collaborative learning, champion teacher-led innovation, and resist the creep of compliance culture into every meeting and conversation. They advocate upward when system settings threaten curiosity, and they model the belief that asking better questions is as important as finding faster answers. In this way, leadership ensures that the canopy is not a fragile decorative layer, but a living, resilient expression of the school's learning culture.

Importantly, curiosity also supports equity. When educators are genuinely curious about students' experiences, strengths, and contexts, they are more likely to adapt practice in ways that meet diverse needs. Inquiry into why certain students are not thriving can surface systemic biases or unexamined assumptions. As such, curiosity becomes not just a learning strategy but a tool for justice.

Curious schools look outward as well as inward. They scan the horizon for new ideas, connect with networks of practice, and contribute to the knowledge base of the profession. They are places of generative learning – where inquiry leads to insight, insight to action, and action to deeper questions.

Finally, the canopy reminds us that flourishing looks different in every school. One school's expression of curiosity may centre on student voice, another on teacher research, another on pedagogical experimentation. What matters is not conformity but coherence. The canopy must grow from the school's roots and trunk – from its moral purpose and capital – not from externally imposed templates.

Curiosity is not the opposite of rigour – it is the pathway to rigour that is relevant, meaningful, and human. It brings schools to life. It reorients improvement around learning, not just performance. And when cultivated intentionally, it builds the resilience, energy, and joy that sustain deep work over time.

It would be tempting to think that this flourishing canopy is the end point of improvement. But in fact, it is only one expression of a much deeper process – a process that must be grown from within. Sustainable change depends not on surface appearance but on coherence from root to branch.

Growth from the inside out: The School Improvement Tree

In many school systems, the improvement journey starts at the canopy – with a preoccupation with what is visible: test scores, public perceptions, surface-level innovation. These efforts often emphasise short-term gains and technical compliance. Leaders are asked to demonstrate rapid impact, and systems measure success through outputs rather than processes. The result is often improvement that is brittle – superficially impressive but vulnerable to stress.

The School Improvement Tree offers a different pathway. It insists that lasting change cannot be achieved by skipping over the roots and trunk. Instead, improvement must begin with clarity of purpose, the development of strong school capital, and a commitment to relational and reflective practice. It is a model that urges schools and systems to grow from the inside out.

Growth from the inside out begins with moral purpose. This is not a mission statement pinned to a wall, but a living set of commitments. Schools must regularly ask: 'What do we stand for? Who do we serve? What does equity look like in our context?' These questions are not rhetorical – they demand courageous reflection and action. Fullan (2011) argues that moral purpose is the driver that connects people to the work at a deeper level. Without it, strategy becomes mechanical. With it, change becomes meaningful.

Clarifying moral purpose is particularly important in times of disruption. In a policy environment that shifts frequently, schools with strong internal clarity are better able to maintain coherence. They do not react impulsively to every new initiative. They engage in principled adaptation – weighing new ideas against their core beliefs and adapting in ways that align with their values and students' needs.

From this foundation, schools must invest in school capital – the intellectual, social, organisational, and financial capacity that enables purpose to be enacted. Too often, reform skips this step. New programs are layered onto already strained systems. Staff are expected to innovate without the time or trust needed to collaborate. Funding is tied to outcomes rather than capacity-building.

Growing from the inside out means prioritising relational infrastructure. Leaders invest in professional learning communities, shared inquiry processes, peer coaching, and open dialogue. Teachers are treated as knowledge builders, not just implementers. Structures support rather than constrain. Time is allocated not only for delivery, but for thinking.

It also means seeing improvement as cumulative, not episodic. Schools that grow from within understand that progress builds over time. They do not expect linear trajectories or overnight transformation. Instead, they look for deepening conversations, stronger relational trust, and expanding capability. They celebrate process as much as product.

This approach does not reject accountability – but it repositions it. Growth from the inside out affirms that external standards and assessments have a role. Data is important. But improvement must be grounded in the school's capacity to learn, adapt, and respond to context. When accountability becomes dislocated from internal capacity, it leads to gaming, compliance, or cynicism. As Hopkins (2024) puts it, 'coherence is the bridge between pressure and support'. Effective systems align expectations with support, and they trust schools to lead their own learning journey.

In practice, this means shifting how systems engage with schools. Rather than mandating top-down programs, systems can ask: 'What are you learning? What are your challenges? How can we help you build the capital needed to grow?' It also means rethinking metrics. Are we measuring what matters? Are we assessing the conditions that make improvement possible – not just the outcomes we hope to see?

Schools that grow from the inside out exhibit several distinctive traits:

- They **value teacher agency**. Staff are involved in setting priorities and designing solutions.
- They **maintain strategic focus**. Initiatives are aligned with a clear vision and implemented with discipline.
- They **treat learning as leadership work**. Leaders model reflection, seek feedback, and build collective capacity.
- They **build resilience**. Change does not collapse when a leader departs or a policy shifts.

Importantly, these schools often innovate from within. Because they understand their context, they are able to create solutions that are both effective and sustainable. Their work may not always be headline-grabbing, but it is coherent and rooted. And over time, it generates trust, improvement, and deeper engagement.

One example might be a school in a low-SES community that chooses to focus on student agency. Rather than importing an external program, it begins by asking students what helps them learn. Teachers collaborate to redesign feedback practices. Time is protected for cross-grade learning walks. The school invests in relational trust, builds its capital, and honours its purpose. The improvement journey is slower – but it sticks.

By contrast, schools that pursue rapid, externally driven reform without building internal coherence often struggle to maintain gains. When the funding ends or leadership changes, practices collapse. What appeared as progress turns out to be unsustained momentum.

Ultimately, growth from the inside out is about integrity – alignment between values, actions, and structures. It requires courage, because it resists the temptation to chase the newest trend or overstate progress. It embraces complexity, because it understands that change is nonlinear. And it centres learning, because it recognises that schools are living systems, not mechanical ones.

When schools grow this way, they become more than organisations. They become communities of purpose. They nurture not just student achievement, but professional pride, ethical commitment, and resilience. And they become capable of sustaining improvement across leadership transitions, policy shifts, and social change.

In the School Improvement Tree, the roots, trunk, and canopy are not isolated parts. They form an ecosystem. And it is from the inside out that this ecosystem thrives.

This is why the School Improvement Tree is not just a metaphor but a practical tool. Schools can use it to guide reflection, align strategy, and shape daily practice. What follows are ways the Tree can be brought to life – in classrooms, across schools, and within systems.

Using the Tree in practice

The School Improvement Tree is more than a metaphor – it is a practical tool that educators and system leaders can use to reflect, plan, and act. Its power lies in its simplicity and flexibility. It offers a shared language for improvement without becoming prescriptive. It is adaptable across contexts, scalable across levels, and grounded in values. Whether used by a classroom teacher, a principal, or a policy team, the Tree provides a structure that supports inquiry, coherence, and growth.

1. As a self-assessment tool

At the school level, the Tree can serve as a diagnostic mirror. Leaders and teams can step back and ask: 'Which parts of the Tree are healthy? Which are underdeveloped?' For example:

- Are our **roots** clear and deep? Do we have a shared sense of purpose that guides our decisions?
- Is our **trunk** strong? Do we have the intellectual, social, organisational, and financial capital to support the work we've committed to?
- Is our **canopy** vibrant? Do we see curiosity, inquiry, and student engagement in classrooms?

This kind of self-assessment is not about judgment – it is about clarity. By mapping current strengths and gaps onto the Tree, schools can better target their efforts. For instance, a school with a strong moral purpose and social capital but weak organisational routines might invest in time structures and team protocols. Another might realise that while systems are sound, purpose has become diluted and needs to be re-centred.

Reflection can be qualitative (for example, staff discussions, focus groups) or scaffolded through surveys or rubrics. Some schools may even co-develop their own indicators for each part of the Tree, ensuring local relevance and ownership.

Considerations could include:

ROOT SYSTEM – moral purpose

Do we have a shared moral compass that guides our work?

Indicator	Reflection questions	Rating / Notes
Shared purpose	Is our moral purpose clear, lived, and visible in daily decisions?	
Equity orientation	Do we prioritise those furthest behind and challenge systemic disadvantage?	
Ethical culture	Are difficult decisions guided by what is right for students – not just what is expedient?	
Leadership alignment	Do leaders model purpose-driven decision-making and relational trust?	
Staff connection to purpose	Do teachers feel connected to the 'why' behind their work?	

TRUNK – school capital

Do we have the capacity and connections to support improvement?

Capital type	Reflection questions	Rating / Notes
Intellectual capital	Do staff have access to relevant knowledge, research, and professional learning?	
Social capital	Is there trust, collaboration, and knowledge sharing across teams?	
Organisational capital	Do we have routines, structures, and time that support professional inquiry?	
Financial capital	Are resources allocated strategically and transparently to reflect our priorities?	

CANOPY – curiosity and outcomes

Are we seeing evidence of curiosity, learning, and thriving in our classrooms?

Indicator	Reflection questions	Rating / Notes
Student engagement	Are students curious, motivated, and able to explore meaningful questions?	
Professional curiosity	Do staff engage in inquiry, challenge assumptions, and seek improvement?	
Adaptive culture	Are we open to experimentation, feedback, and learning from mistakes?	
Outcome diversity	Do we value growth, wellbeing, creativity, and citizenship alongside achievement?	
Equity of impact	Are our outcomes improving most for those historically underserved?	

2. As a strategic framework

The Tree can also be used as a strategic planning frame. Rather than listing isolated initiatives, leaders can map each strategy to a part of the Tree:

- Does this new literacy intervention **deepen our roots** by aligning with our belief in equity?
- Does our professional development **strengthen the trunk** by building collective knowledge and trust?
- Will this inquiry-based unit **expand the canopy** by fostering student agency and curiosity?

This approach prevents scattergun implementation and encourages coherence. It reminds leaders to balance their focus – not to overemphasise one part of the Tree at the expense of others. For example, efforts to drive curiosity (canopy) will fail if staff don't have time or structures to collaborate (trunk). Conversely, investing in capital without a unifying purpose may lead to activity without direction.

Strategic use of the Tree ensures that improvement is aligned, layered, and purposeful. It also makes school plans more accessible – staff, students, and families can more easily engage with a model that is visual, relational, and intuitive. Considerations could include:

ROOT SYSTEM – moral purpose

Anchor decisions in equity, service, and shared ethical commitment.

Strategic priority	Example initiative	Reflection questions	Intended impact
Deepen moral purpose	Rearticulate the school's values with staff, students, and families	Does this clarify *why* we do what we do? Are all voices represented in this conversation?	Stronger alignment between strategy and values
Strengthen equity lens	Establish an Equity Action Team to review inclusion practices	Does this initiative centre those furthest behind?	More inclusive practices and equitable resource allocation
Build purpose into routines	Embed student voice into staff meetings and planning	Are we listening to students when making decisions that affect them?	A more democratic, purpose-driven school culture

TRUNK – school capital

Ensure the enabling conditions are in place for sustained professional growth and collective capacity.

Strategic priority	Example initiative	Reflection questions	Intended impact
Build intellectual capital	Introduce collaborative inquiry cycles focused on high-impact practice	Are we building collective expertise, not just individual skill?	Improved teaching quality and shared instructional language
Strengthen social capital	Create cross-team coaching partnerships	Will this build trust and collaborative momentum?	Greater professional trust and knowledge exchange
Enhance organisational capital	Redesign meeting structures to prioritise deep collaboration and reflection	Does our use of time reflect our values?	Time and space for adult learning aligned with school goals
Align financial capital	Reallocate discretionary funding to support teacher-led inquiry	Are we resourcing what matters most?	Investment in staff agency and innovative practice

CANOPY – curiosity and student outcomes

Foster vibrant, engaged learning where students and staff can thrive.

Strategic priority	Example initiative	Reflection questions	Intended impact
Elevate student agency	Co-design inquiry units with student input	Does this foster curiosity, voice, and ownership?	Higher engagement and deeper learning
Nurture staff curiosity	Offer opt-in professional learning based on teacher inquiry interests	Are we supporting professional curiosity, not just compliance?	Increased intrinsic motivation and innovation
Broaden definition of success	Redesign reporting to include creativity, collaboration and wellbeing	Do our outcomes reflect what we truly value?	A richer, more holistic view of student growth
Build learning culture	Establish regular 'showcase' exhibitions of student work	Do we celebrate curiosity and meaningful learning publicly?	Greater pride, authenticity, and visibility of student effort

3. As a professional learning lens

For teacher teams and middle leaders, the Tree offers a valuable **professional learning lens**. It can frame inquiry cycles, team reflections, or coaching conversations. A team might ask:

- How are our routines supporting or hindering collaboration?
- Where is student curiosity evident in our lessons?
- Are our practices consistent with our stated moral purpose?

The Tree helps educators see the connections between their daily work and broader school culture. It also opens space for adaptive problem-solving. If students are disengaged, the answer may not lie in classroom technique alone – it may point to deeper issues in school culture, leadership expectations, or time use. The Tree helps teams see beyond symptoms to causes.

Some schools use the metaphor to shape internal PD – structuring staff days around root (purpose), trunk (capacity), and canopy (practice) themes. Others design their improvement goals around each part of the Tree, ensuring a holistic development pathway.

Considerations might include:

Part of the Tree	Guiding focus	Reflective questions for teams and leaders	Professional learning applications
Roots – moral purpose	Anchor learning in shared values and ethical intent	• Are our current practices consistent with our values? • Do our pedagogical choices reflect a belief in equity and inclusion? • Is our professional learning guided by what matters most for students?	• Begin inquiry cycles with reflection on purpose • Revisit the school vision to frame learning goals • Use staff meetings to explore ethical dilemmas in practice
Trunk – school capital	Strengthen the conditions for growth and collaboration	• Do we have time and structures that support shared learning? • Are we building trust and professional relationships across teams? • Is new knowledge being spread or siloed?	• Audit staff meeting structures to prioritise collaboration • Use coaching and peer observation to grow social and intellectual capital • Align PD resourcing with identified staff learning needs
Canopy – curiosity and practice	Focus on student engagement, teacher inquiry, and visible learning	• Where is student curiosity evident in our classrooms? • Are teachers engaging in professional inquiry? • Are our practices fostering deep thinking, agency, and joy in learning?	• Analyse student work through a curiosity lens • Co-design inquiry units that centre on student questions • Offer opt-in PD based on teacher-generated problems of practice

4. As a system diagnostic

At the regional or system level, the Tree can function as a diagnostic and design tool. It invites systems to ask not only 'What are schools doing?' but 'What are we enabling?' For example:

- Are funding models supporting capital growth or short-term outputs?
- Do policy settings encourage clarity of purpose or reactive compliance?
- Are networks focused on shared inquiry or on performative benchmarking?

By applying the Tree across schools or clusters, systems can identify patterns. If multiple schools lack a strong trunk, it may indicate the need for investment in leadership development or collaborative structures. If curiosity is consistently absent, systems may need to revisit curriculum flexibility, assessment models, or professional autonomy.

The Tree allows system leaders to shift from mandate to enablement – from telling schools what to do to helping them become what they need to be.

In all these applications, the Tree invites adaptive leadership. It does not offer a checklist or silver bullet. It embraces nuance, welcomes reflection, and insists on coherence. It reminds us that real improvement is not linear – it is layered, relational, and rooted. And it calls for care as well as courage.

Considerations might include:

Part of the Tree	System-level focus	Guiding questions
Roots – moral purpose	Align policy with shared ethical commitments and long-term vision	• Do our strategies reflect a coherent moral purpose – or fragmented priorities? • Are we asking schools to align with values we haven't clearly articulated? • Do leaders have the space and language to discuss purpose openly?
Trunk – school capital	Build and sustain the enabling conditions for school growth	• Are funding models fostering long-term investment or short-term compliance? • Do leadership development programs grow social and organisational capital? • Are networks and professional learning communities enabling knowledge sharing and trust?
Canopy – curiosity and learning outcomes	Promote a culture of inquiry, innovation, and deep learning	• Are curriculum settings flexible enough to support teacher and student curiosity? • Is assessment policy reinforcing compliance or opening space for creativity? • Are schools rewarded for authentic learning growth – or narrow performance?

But not all trees grow in fertile soil. The work of school improvement becomes even more vital – and more challenging – in communities facing deep disadvantage. The next chapter turns to this question: how can schools nurture growth when conditions are harsh?

Looking ahead: growing in difficult soil

The School Improvement Tree offers a hopeful model for sustainable change – but not all schools grow in fertile conditions. In many communities, the soil is dry. The challenges are complex and layered: intergenerational poverty, policy instability, fractured services, historical marginalisation, and social inequity. These are the schools that operate in difficult soil – where the ground is uneven, the weather unpredictable, and the nutrients not evenly distributed.

The next chapter explores what it means to grow the Tree in these harsh conditions. It focuses on schools serving communities marked by systemic disadvantage – where instability, under-resourcing, and low expectations have become part of the landscape. These are not schools in need of saving. They are schools in need of belief, support, and the tools to grow from within.

In such contexts, the Tree must adapt. Growth is still possible – in fact, it is perhaps more essential here than anywhere else. But it demands different conditions, different leadership, and deeper commitment. The roots of moral purpose must go even deeper. In the face of inequity, schools must hold fast to values of justice, inclusion, and care. They must become not just places of instruction, but anchors of dignity and belief in young people's potential.

The trunk – school capital – must be consciously and deliberately strengthened. There is no margin for waste or fragmentation. Every resource matters. Every relationship counts. Building intellectual, social, organisational, and financial capital becomes not a luxury but a lifeline. The work must be collaborative, strategic, and sustained.

And the canopy of curiosity must be fiercely protected. In environments that too often erode wonder – where student agency is undermined by trauma, and where teacher energy is depleted by stress – curiosity becomes a radical act. To encourage inquiry, dialogue, exploration, and joy in learning is to affirm that all young people deserve more than survival. They deserve to thrive.

This next chapter will not offer easy solutions. But it will share how schools in challenging settings can – and do – grow. Their stories show that adversity does not preclude transformation. But it does demand intention, courage, and care.

From insight to action: growth from the inside out

The School Improvement Tree offers not just a metaphor for understanding growth, but a practical guide for shaping it. The following prompts invite teachers, principals, and system leaders to bring the Tree to life – through everyday choices that deepen purpose, strengthen capital, and cultivate curiosity.

For teachers:

- Reflect on how your daily practice nurtures both strong roots (purpose) and a flourishing canopy (curiosity and outcomes).
- Map a recent unit or project against the Tree – where did moral purpose show through? Where was student curiosity invited? Where did capital support or limit growth?
- Share with colleagues one small way you are helping to 'grow the trunk' through collaborative practice or building social capital.

For principals:

- Use the Tree metaphor in leadership conversations to frame the balance between purpose, capital, and curiosity.
- Diagnose your school's current growth. Are the roots deep enough? Is the trunk strong and healthy? Is the canopy diverse and dynamic?
- Protect time and space for collective inquiry – ensure it is a regular rhythm, not an occasional event.
- Encourage leadership at all levels to identify where they can invest in strengthening the trunk (professional trust, social learning networks, infrastructure that supports agency).

For systems:

- Shift from program delivery to enabling growth – use the Tree to guide policy conversations about what sustainable improvement requires.
- Analyse system levers: are they nurturing deep purpose, building capital, and protecting curiosity? Where are they inadvertently stifling growth?
- Use the Tree metaphor to challenge deficit narratives – especially in low-SES contexts – by focusing on growth potential rather than gaps.
- Ensure that networks, funding models, and accountability processes enable rather than crowd out deep learning.

A healthy Tree grows from the inside out. The next step is not more programs but stronger roots, a sturdier trunk, and a more vibrant canopy. Choose where to start nurturing today.

The Cat climbs higher. The branches hold firm. The canopy rustles – not with answers, but with questions. A learning breeze stirs the system. Something vital is growing – again.

Afterword: the tree as a way forward

The School Improvement Tree is not a diagram to be filled in or a checklist to be completed. It is an invitation - to see schools not as mechanisms to be fixed but as living systems to be nurtured. Growth does not always look dramatic. Sometimes it is slow. Sometimes it is hidden beneath the surface. But when rooted in purpose, supported by capital, and crowned with curiosity, growth becomes inevitable.

Each part of the Tree matters. Neglect one, and the others suffer. Strengthen one, and the whole system responds. It is in the interaction - between roots, trunk, and canopy - that learning flourishes and community deepens.

The Tree is also a mirror. It reflects the values we prioritise, the systems we sustain, and the questions we are willing to ask. And perhaps most importantly, it reminds us that in education, nothing grows well without care.

Let this metaphor travel with you - not as a model to impose, but as a lens to interpret, adapt, and personalise. Let it provoke questions, guide decisions, and centre what matters most.

Because in every school, something is already growing. The question is: what are we tending, and what are we letting wither?

The School Improvement Tree offers more than a metaphor; it provides a practical framework for understanding how moral purpose, school capital, and curiosity interact to support sustainable growth. But its value lies not only in shaping general improvement efforts - it also offers a lens for tackling some of the most entrenched challenges in education.

The next chapter asks how this model can help address one of education's most persistent challenges: the impact of socioeconomic inequality on student learning - and how curiosity, moral purpose, and school capital can work to disrupt it.

And if you look closely - just beyond the roots, between the branches, or under the canopy - you might spot the Curious Cat. Never far away, always watching, always wondering. Not to offer answers, but to remind us to keep asking better questions. Because that's where real growth begins.

CHAPTER 7

Through the Socioeconomic Shadow – Curiosity and Equity

BIG IDEAS IN THIS CHAPTER

Socioeconomic status (SES) remains the most powerful predictor of student outcomes. This chapter explores how deeply inequity is embedded – and how systems have failed to shift it.

Disadvantage is not just material – it becomes cultural. Expectations, beliefs, and opportunities are shaped by what students and teachers see around them every day.

Curiosity is not a luxury – it's a lifeline. In high-pressure, low-SES settings, fostering inquiry is an act of resistance and hope.

Schools can't eliminate inequality alone – but they can interrupt its reproduction. Moral purpose, strong capital, and curiosity create cultures where students defy the odds.

This chapter asks:

- How does your school confront disadvantage – not just with programs, but with mindset and mission?
- What would it take to make curiosity equitable, not exclusive?

'Justice is what love looks like in public.' – Cornel West

The uneven starting line

The link between SES and student achievement is not a newly discovered challenge – it has been documented, debated, and dissected in policy reports, academic studies, and parliamentary inquiries for decades. One of the earliest and most influential was the *Equality of Educational Opportunity* study (Coleman et al., 1966), which concluded that student background – especially family SES – was more strongly associated with achievement than any single school-level variable. While often interpreted as a sign that schools don't matter, later work reframed this to suggest that schools *can* make a difference, particularly when they focus on building professional capital, strengthening leadership, and fostering cultures of inquiry.

Yet despite this extensive attention, it remains unresolved. The persistence of this problem is not due to a lack of knowledge – we have decades of research, inquiries, and international comparisons pointing to the same core issues – but to a failure of implementation, coherence, and sustained commitment. Promising insights are too often lost in translation between research and practice, fragmented across initiatives, or diluted by short-term policy cycles. The system's architecture is frequently misaligned: funding models, curriculum demands, workforce strategies, and accountability mechanisms pull in different directions, creating friction rather than flow. As a result, well-evidenced ideas fail to gain traction, and deep inequities remain stubbornly intact – not because we don't know what to do, but because we haven't found the collective will, capacity, or coherence to do it at scale and over time.

Stephen Lamb and colleagues (2020) highlight 'a consistent failure to translate evidence into system-wide impact, especially for the most disadvantaged learners'.

In Australia, schools serving low-SES communities often operate under immense pressure. They are expected to 'close the gap', meet national standards, and improve NAPLAN results, often without the support or conditions necessary to sustain that improvement. The result is a kind of policy fatigue – a sense that every few years brings another plan, another framework, another set of metrics, but little lasting change. Lingard et al. (2014) argue that data infrastructures in education have too often narrowed what counts as success, privileging test performance over deep learning, and discouraging the kind of curiosity that leads to innovation.

> ### Vignette: Building culture not prisons
>
> *A story of how school leaders protected trust and curiosity in a community under pressure.*
>
> In two remote P–12 schools in eastern Victoria, where native logging is shutting down and the local economy is unravelling, school has become more than a place of education – it's a stabilising force in a fraying community. Both towns are small. Everyone knows everyone. And in both schools, the principals are deeply embedded in local life. They lead not just institutions, but identities.
>
> On paper, the schools are strong. NAPLAN performance is steady. Senior students achieve solid ATAR results. However, attendance can be erratic at times, unsurprisingly, reflecting communities where challenges can include entrenched disadvantage, family instability, generational trauma, and a community adjusting to the slow collapse of its economic heart.
>
> The department's most recent intervention was an 'attendance fidelity' approach – meant to ensure attendance data is 100 per cent accurate. 'It felt like they wanted us to build a better prison,' one principal remarked. 'But our job is to keep building a school – a place kids want to come back to, not be locked into.'
>
> So that's what they're doing: investing in relationships, anchoring culture, and leading with moral clarity. Not because it's easy, but because it matters. In the absence of system solutions, they've become the system that works. The lesson? When policy misreads context, it's the culture of the school – and the curiosity and commitment of its people – that carries the work forward.

Teachers in these schools frequently carry a dual burden: the emotional labour of supporting students living with trauma, poverty, or instability, and the bureaucratic weight of external accountability regimes. These demands are not trivial. They shape the way teachers perceive their work, and over time they can suppress the very dispositions – curiosity, creativity, empathy – that make teaching transformative.

Compounding these pressures is the reality that staff turnover is higher in low-SES schools, with early-career teachers often placed in the most challenging contexts without the mentoring and professional learning they need (OECD, 2019a). This churn disrupts continuity, undermines collective expertise, and reinforces a cycle where the most vulnerable students are least likely to experience sustained, high-quality instruction. Even when well-intentioned programs are introduced, their impact is often blunted by inconsistency in leadership, limited buy-in from staff, or the exhaustion of constantly responding to external mandates.

Lamb et al.'s (2020) analysis highlights how students in disadvantaged communities are more likely to attend schools with fewer experienced teachers, higher student/teacher ratios, lower access to support services, and weaker networks of academic capital. The consequence is not only lower achievement, but also diminished belief – among students and staff – that learning can be joyful, inquiry-driven, and relevant. In this way, disadvantage becomes not just a material condition but a cultural one, shaping what is expected, imagined, and pursued.

Despite this, some schools resist the gravity of disadvantage. They don't ignore the structural barriers – but neither do they allow those barriers to define their trajectory. These schools become what David Hopkins (2007) described as 'intelligent schools' – organisations that learn from themselves and from one another, that reflect on practice and adapt with intent. What distinguishes these schools is not a single program or leadership model, but a culture of inquiry rooted in shared moral purpose.

In these schools, curiosity is not a luxury – it is a lifeline. It provides the energy to ask: What's really going on here? Why do some students disengage while others thrive? What can we learn from those moments when things go well? These are not compliance-driven questions. They are learning questions – questions that invite educators into a deeper understanding of their students and their practice.

Crucially, these schools also seek coherence, not compliance. They align their strategies with their values, using data not to rank but to reflect. They create routines that support collective learning – structured inquiry cycles, peer observation, learning walks – and protect time for those routines to take root. They talk openly about complexity, about failure, about moments of joy. And they engage with families and communities not just as stakeholders but as partners in the work of improvement.

One such example is a cluster of schools in a large metropolitan region that initiated their own inquiry-based improvement network. Principals and teachers from each school came together every six weeks to share puzzles of practice, interrogate student learning samples, and collaborate on responsive strategies. The focus was not on competition or compliance, but on building trust, deepening professional capital, and sharing responsibility for student growth. What emerged was a culture of mutual learning – one that was more resilient, adaptive, and equitable.

The enduring challenge of SES-related inequality, then, is not simply a problem to be solved with better data or more funding. It is a question of culture and capability. It requires systems and schools to develop the professional capital, collaborative infrastructure, and moral clarity to respond with curiosity rather than control.

To shift from knowing to doing – from research to reform – requires what Michael Fullan (2015) calls 'systemness': a recognition that improvement is not the job of isolated actors but a collective responsibility shared across roles, schools, and sectors. It also requires humility: the willingness to admit that what we've done so far has not been enough, and the courage to imagine something different.

Yet even when schools hold moral purpose and capability in mind, one of the most insidious forces working against equity is the hidden cost of performative pressure – the way external demands distort culture and narrow curiosity.

The hidden cost of performative pressure

In many low-SES schools, the daily work of teaching and leading takes place under the shadow of performative accountability. While public reporting, school improvement plans, and standardised testing are intended to promote transparency and drive progress, they often create a climate in which surface-level compliance is rewarded more than authentic learning. When teachers and leaders feel that their professional worth is measured solely through performance metrics – particularly those disconnected from context – the deeper work of inquiry, collaboration, and relationship-building can be crowded out (Lingard, 2010).

This performativity is not unique to disadvantaged schools, but it hits them hardest. In schools already navigating complexity – poverty, mobility, trauma, and limited community resources – the demand to produce neat data narratives can feel like an added injustice. Rather than encouraging reflection, external pressures may compel schools to focus narrowly on what can be measured, often at the expense of what matters most. The result is a kind of educational myopia: attention is directed toward test preparation, superficial goal-setting, and 'evidence' that conforms to system expectations rather than local realities (Mockler, 2011).

The consequences are tangible. Curriculum narrows. Professional learning becomes instrumental. Teaching becomes more scripted. Creative risk-taking declines. And worst of all, curiosity – with all its generative potential – starts to seem like a liability rather than a strength. Educators may begin to believe that asking deeper questions, exploring new approaches, or challenging the status quo is risky, even unprofessional. In such contexts, compliance masquerades as improvement.

This can lead to what Berliner (2006) calls 'instructional triage' – a practice in which educators are forced to focus their energy on the students and areas that will most directly impact performance metrics, often to the detriment of broader educational engagement. In some schools, this has meant pulling resources away from inquiry-based learning, interdisciplinary projects, or pastoral care in order to double down on literacy and numeracy drills for students 'on the cusp'.

Obviously, no school should be discouraged from pursuing excellence, but the question is: excellence for whom, and defined by what? When equity is framed through a purely performative lens, the deeper work of transformation – rebuilding trust, rethinking pedagogy, engaging families, cultivating professional learning communities – is pushed aside. And when the voices of students, families, and educators are excluded from the improvement conversation, we risk reinforcing the very inequities we seek to dismantle.

Curious schools take a different path. They acknowledge the demands of external accountability but refuse to let them dictate the culture of the school. Instead of chasing numbers, they pursue meaning. Instead of short-term compliance, they invest in long-term growth. They treat data as one source of insight – not the only one – and they work to build a rich evidence base that includes student voice, teacher reflection, peer observation, and shared inquiry.

In these schools, leadership plays a pivotal role – not through top-down control, but by modelling curiosity, protecting professional space, and building trust in collective inquiry.

One school in a disadvantaged metropolitan community made a deliberate choice to counteract performative pressure by redefining success around engagement, agency, and connection. The leadership team introduced protocols for student-led conferences, encouraged staff to document learning through narrative observations, and established weekly inquiry sessions where teachers presented puzzles of practice. While their NAPLAN data did not immediately shift, suspension rates dropped, student attendance improved, and staff retention stabilised. Over time, deeper learning gains followed.

This approach requires courage – especially in systems where funding, status, and legitimacy are closely tied to test scores. But it also requires trust: trust in teachers to make sound professional judgments, trust in leaders to frame accountability in developmental terms, and trust in students to engage when learning is meaningful. Without this trust, performativity becomes a barrier to genuine improvement.

Ultimately, the cost of performative pressure is not just professional – it is human. It undermines the relationships that anchor good teaching, the autonomy that fuels professional growth, and the curiosity that makes learning possible. Equity work cannot thrive in a culture of fear. It needs space, time, and permission to ask difficult questions.

As this chapter argues, curiosity is not a soft virtue. It is a hard necessity. Especially in contexts of disadvantage, it provides the entry point for honest reflection, adaptive practice, and relational leadership. To protect and nurture curiosity is not to reject accountability – it is to reclaim the deeper purpose of schooling.

Reclaiming agency in schools

In disadvantaged communities, it is tempting to see schools as recipients of external policy, funding, and direction – as places where systems intervene, rather than where agency resides. But the most effective and resilient schools in low-SES contexts invert that narrative. They do not wait for rescue. They act with purpose, confidence, and coherence. They become sites of collective agency, where professional judgment is valued, inquiry is embedded, and improvement grows from within.

Agency in this context does not mean autonomy in the narrow managerial sense. It means the ability of educators to shape their work, respond to their students, and collaborate around shared questions. Priestley et al. (2015) argue that teacher agency is a capacity developed through supportive structures, meaningful professional relationships, and an environment that values professional voice. When those conditions are met, schools become more than delivery mechanisms – they become learning communities.

Curious schools in low-SES settings understand that agency is both a right and a responsibility. They invest in relational trust. They protect time for collaborative inquiry. They create systems where teachers and leaders do not merely implement change – they design it, monitor it, and adapt it in real time.

In one P-12 college, the leadership team shifted from top-down mandates to distributed leadership through instructional coaching and action research. Teachers were invited to identify a puzzle of practice, explore it with colleagues, gather data, and share findings. Over time, these inquiries coalesced into school-wide themes: improving formative assessment, enhancing feedback, deepening student voice. Staff began to feel not only heard but influential. As one teacher put it, 'This isn't just PD anymore – it's our work.'

In such schools, leadership is not a title but a function distributed across the organisation. Middle leaders become catalysts for inquiry, mentors become co-learners, and professional learning becomes embedded in the flow of daily practice. The result is a form of grassroots improvement – rooted in context, responsive to need, and sustained by shared commitment.

Importantly, these schools resist the binary between compliance and chaos. They understand the need for structure and coherence, but they shape those frameworks around their local values and goals. They see external demands not as scripts to follow but as provocations to engage with critically. In doing so, they reclaim improvement as a generative process – not an imposed checklist.

This sense of ownership extends to students and families as well. In many curious schools, agency is not limited to staff – it is shared with the community. Students are invited into planning conversations, school reviews include family perspectives, and decisions about wellbeing and pedagogy are informed by those most affected. This approach is not about consultation alone – it is about co-construction. It reflects what Smyth (2011) calls 'deliberative democracy in schooling' – a practice that strengthens equity by redistributing voice and responsibility.

Families are engaged not only as stakeholders but as contributors to the school's culture of curiosity – helping frame questions about learning, community wellbeing, and shared aspiration.

The result is a school culture that feels less like a hierarchy and more like a network of learners: a place where change is not driven from above but shaped from within, where improvement is not episodic but ongoing, and where curiosity – rather than compliance – becomes the engine of collective action.

Schools as sites of agency offer a powerful counter-narrative to the story of deficit and dependency that often surrounds disadvantaged communities. They demonstrate that while context matters, so does culture; that while resources are critical, so too is respect; and that equity is not just about redistribution – it is about recognition and participation.

Curious schools do not deny the complexity of their work. They lean into it – with questions, with courage, and with collective will. They remind us that equity does not arrive fully formed from a policy office. It is built, tested, and refined every day in the choices educators make together.

Curiosity as a disruptive force for equity

In a system that too often reinforces inequality – through funding disparities, stratified enrolment patterns, and deficit assumptions – curiosity offers a quiet but radical form of resistance. It invites educators to look again at what they think they know, to question inherited narratives, and to see their students not through the lens of limitation but through the possibilities of potential. In this way, curiosity becomes more than a pedagogical tool – it becomes a disruptive force for equity.

Disruption, in this sense, is not about chaos or rebellion. It is about loosening the grip of assumptions that bind practice to past patterns. It is about interrupting habitual responses – such as the belief that some students are 'too far behind', or that poor behaviour reflects a lack of motivation rather than unmet needs. Curiosity challenges these stories. It replaces judgment with inquiry.

When teachers are encouraged to ask deeper questions – about what students are experiencing, what might be working, and what they could try differently – practice shifts. Pedagogy becomes more responsive. Relationships strengthen. And classrooms become spaces not just of transmission but of transformation. Delpit (2006) reminds educators that equity is not about lowering expectations but about finding better ways to meet them.

Curious schools make this visible. They design inquiry-based learning that allows students to pursue authentic questions, connect with their communities, and express their identities. They embed curiosity in teaching practice – through protocols for reflection, cycles of action research, and collaborative planning. And they model it in leadership – by inviting feedback, surfacing dilemmas, and holding space for ambiguity.

One primary school in a low-income urban area introduced 'learning provocations' at the start of each week – open-ended questions tied to real-world issues. Students responded through writing, discussion, and projects. Teachers then built their curriculum plans around the ideas and interests that emerged. Over time, students who had previously been disengaged became active participants. They recognised themselves in the learning and saw that their voices mattered. Teachers, in turn, reported greater professional fulfilment and stronger cross-disciplinary collaboration.

In this way, curiosity shifts the locus of control. It decentralises knowledge. It opens learning to co-construction. And it reminds everyone – students, staff, and families – that education is not a script to follow, but a conversation to join.

This is especially powerful in communities that have been historically marginalised. Curiosity validates lived experience. It affirms that knowing does not reside only in textbooks or experts. It lives in stories, questions, and relationships. And when schools treat those stories as sources of insight – not problems to fix – they begin to build the trust that equity requires.

Importantly, this kind of curiosity is disciplined. It is not idle speculation or 'anything goes' exploration. It is purposeful, moral, and grounded in the work of improvement. It asks, for example:

- Why are some of our students thriving while others are not?
- How do our practices, policies, or assumptions contribute to the patterns we see?
- What are we learning from our students that challenges us to do better?

These are not easy questions. But they are essential. They create the conditions for adaptive expertise – what Timperley et al. (2014) describe as the capacity to inquire into impact and adjust practice in response.

Curiosity also helps to sustain momentum. In many low-SES schools, hope is fragile. Change can be slow, and setbacks common. But when educators remain curious – about what's working, about what's possible, about what matters – they are better able to persist. They are more likely to see progress in unexpected places and to keep learning even in the face of uncertainty.

In this sense, curiosity is both a mindset and a mechanism. It fuels the professional energy needed to do equity work well. It fosters the collective reflection required to make change meaningful. And it creates a culture where improvement is not something done *to* teachers or *for* students – but *with* them.

Aligning system conditions with moral purpose

If curiosity is the engine of equity, moral purpose is its compass. It provides direction, coherence, and resolve. Without a strong sense of why – of what schools are for – curiosity can drift, become performative, or serve narrow ends. But when moral purpose is clear and collective, it anchors inquiry in something deeper than technique. It ensures that curiosity is not just a classroom strategy, but a whole-system ethic.

Michael Fullan (2003) defines moral purpose as the intention to make a positive difference in the lives of all students, especially those who have been historically underserved. In low-SES schools, moral purpose often takes the form of quiet tenacity: teachers who show up every day for students who have been let down before, leaders who refuse to lower expectations despite public cynicism, and teams who choose collaboration over blame. Moral purpose in these contexts is not lofty idealism – it is grounded, gritty, and sustained by trust.

But moral purpose alone is not enough. To thrive, it must be supported by system conditions that enable professional growth, protect reflective time, and value relational practice. Unfortunately, too many schools operate in systems that undermine these conditions. Rapid policy churn, high-stakes accountability, and fragmented initiatives make it difficult for moral purpose to take root. David Hopkins (2020) notes that reform without coherence tends to produce superficial change – compliance without commitment.

Curious schools need systems that are designed for learning, not just delivery. This means:

- **Allocating time** for professional inquiry and collaborative planning
- **Providing coaching and mentoring** that supports adaptive, not just technical, expertise
- **Recognising diverse forms of evidence**, including student voice, narrative data, and teacher reflection
- **Fostering networks** of schools that share learning, not just compare performance
- **Stabilising policy frameworks** to allow local innovation to mature.

Systems also need to acknowledge the emotional dimensions of equity work. Sustained engagement with disadvantage is not simply a cognitive task – it is relational, affective, and often confronting. Educators working in high-need schools require not only resources but emotional support, psychological safety, and permission to share their doubts and discoveries without fear of judgment. When systems fail to provide this, burnout rises and morale erodes.

A system oriented toward curiosity and moral purpose is one that trusts its educators, not blindly but wisely. It invests in leadership development. It learns from schools on the edge, not just the centre. And it avoids the trap of scaling one-size-fits-all models by instead scaling the capacity for local inquiry.

This kind of system leadership is slow, relational, and deeply human. It takes seriously the complexity of educational work, especially in communities affected by socioeconomic disadvantage. It treats equity not as a target, but as a process – a series of deliberate choices about how time, talent, and trust are distributed.

To create these conditions, system leaders must be learners too. They must ask:

- How do our policies support or suppress school-level curiosity?
- Are we rewarding what matters, or what is easy to measure?
- What do we learn when we listen to the schools most affected by disadvantage?

When systems model the inquiry they ask of schools, coherence grows. So does confidence. And in that environment, curiosity is not a risk – it is a resource.

But creating enabling system conditions is not enough – curiosity and moral purpose must still be protected daily within the life of each school. The final challenge is sustaining wonder where the pressures are greatest.

Holding the line on wonder

The link between SES and achievement is not inevitable. It is historical, structural, and deeply human – but it is not fixed. Schools and systems have a choice: to reinforce the patterns of the past, or to cultivate the dispositions that lead to something better. The shadow of inequality is long, but it is not unchangeable. It can be challenged – not only by better funding or stronger policies, but by a cultural shift toward curiosity, moral purpose, and school capital as drivers of improvement.

Curiosity, when intentionally embedded in the professional life of a school, becomes more than a practice – it becomes a stance. It invites educators to slow down, to notice patterns, and to reflect before reacting. It asks teachers to wonder, 'What else could be true?' and to resist the flattening logic of data alone. It strengthens their capacity to listen – to students, to families, to each other – and to use what they hear as a prompt for action. In this way, curiosity is not just how schools learn – it is how they change.

Yet the conditions that support this kind of learning are fragile. In schools serving high-need communities, the urgency of daily demands can easily overwhelm reflective space. Leaders under pressure may feel the pull toward technical solutions and linear outcomes. Teachers facing exhaustion may default to routine. System actors seeking quick wins may undervalue slow work. This is the reality in which equity work must take place – and it is why holding the line on wonder is so critical.

Sustaining curiosity also depends on staff continuity – when leadership and teaching teams churn frequently, trust erodes and the habits of inquiry struggle to take hold.

Holding the line means protecting the moments when real learning happens. It means safeguarding time for reflection, resisting the pressure to simplify complexity, and defending professional relationships from fragmentation. It means choosing, again and again, to see students not as gaps to close but as minds to ignite. It is a practice of faith – in each other, in the profession, and in the possibility that things can be otherwise.

This chapter has shown that curiosity is not ornamental. It is not a distraction from the 'real work' of schooling. It is the real work – particularly in communities where the stakes are high and the margin for error is slim. It is the thread that connects purpose to practice, equity to action. And when joined with strong moral foundations and well-developed capital, it offers a framework for both resisting inequality and reimagining what schools can be.

These ideas are not theoretical. They are visible in the work of educators across Australia who choose daily to ask rather than assume, to connect rather than withdraw, to teach with imagination rather than instruction alone. In doing so, they change the trajectory not only of their schools but of the young people who walk through their doors. They remind us that education is, at its best, a project of hope – one built on questions, not answers.

To hold the line on wonder – in the face of pressure, complexity, and fatigue – is not naïve. It is the work. And it is among the most important work we can do.

Because the work is not done. And neither is the Cat.

From insight to action: curiosity and equity in schooling

Through the socioeconomic shadow, curiosity, moral purpose, and school capital offer not simple solutions but pathways to sustained, equitable improvement. The reflections and actions below invite teachers, principals, and system leaders to move from insight to agency – creating schools where curiosity and moral purpose actively disrupt the patterns of disadvantage.

For teachers:

- Create classroom cultures where all students' questions and experiences are valued.
- Embed inquiry-based learning that connects with students' lives and communities.
- Reflect on whose voices and cultural perspectives are represented in your curriculum.
- Notice barriers to curiosity in your classroom – rigid pacing, over-reliance on testing, deficit assumptions – and gently subvert them.

For principals:

- Name equity as a shared moral purpose with staff – keep it visible in decision-making.
- Protect professional learning time for inquiry into equity-related challenges.
- Map patterns of access, participation, and success in your school – who is thriving, and who is not?
- Foster partnerships with families and community leaders as co-educators, not just stakeholders.

For systems:

- Frame curiosity and moral purpose as drivers of system-wide equity – not as 'soft' or peripheral values.
- Create funding, staffing, and accountability policies that enable rather than constrain schools serving disadvantaged communities.
- Encourage networked learning – support school leaders to collaborate on problems of practice around equity.
- Audit system processes to identify where they inadvertently reproduce disadvantage.

In the shadow of disadvantage, it is curiosity, shared purpose, and collective agency that cast the first light. The work begins, and continues, with the courage to ask: what more is possible here?

And the Curious Cat knows this. It walks the fence line of the school, pausing not to solve but to notice. It peers into classrooms where questions bloom and staffrooms where laughter returns. It lingers where leaders listen and students lean in. It waits, not for applause but for the next question worth asking.

Afterword: the Cat beneath the shadow

Leadership plays a pivotal role in sustaining this work. While frameworks and networks matter, it is leaders – at every level – who shape the daily culture of schools and systems. They model the curiosity they wish to see, create the trust conditions in which inquiry can thrive, and help align curiosity with moral purpose. The next chapter explores how curiosity can shape the craft of leadership – building cultures of inquiry, equity, and innovation across schools and systems.

Chapter 8 explores this craft of leadership in depth – showing how curiosity is not only sustained by leaders but embodied as a defining characteristic of how they learn, lead, and drive change.

The Curious Cat lingers in the margins – where the policies fade and the real work begins. It does not flinch at complexity. It prowls the schoolyard with quiet confidence, not to escape the shadow of disadvantage but to learn how light might break through it.

It sits beside the teacher pausing to ask, 'What am I missing?' It watches the student who, for the first time, dares to wonder aloud. It follows the leader who chooses to listen before solving. It knows that equity is not achieved in declarations, but in the slow, human work of noticing, asking, and learning again.

And it knows – better than most – that some of the best questions live in the places we're most afraid to look.

CHAPTER 8

Leading for Inquiry, Equity, and Change

BIG IDEAS IN THIS CHAPTER

Leadership is not about answers – it's about the courage to ask better questions. Curious leaders lead with humility, openness, and a commitment to collective learning.

The most powerful change agents listen before they act. This chapter explores how inquiry-driven leadership strengthens trust, collaboration, and creativity.

Curiosity shifts culture. When leaders model curiosity, they foster psychological safety, moral purpose, and deeper learning in their teams.

The best leadership practices are often quiet, relational, and unfinished. Adaptive, responsive leadership makes room for uncertainty – and grows stronger through it.

This chapter asks:

- How do you lead when you don't know the answer?
- How might curiosity transform not just your leadership style – but the system you lead within?

'Be patient toward all that is unsolved in your heart and try to love the questions themselves.' – Rainer Maria Rilke

The power of leading with questions

Leadership in education has long been associated with vision, authority, and decisiveness. But in a rapidly changing world, it is increasingly defined by something less certain and more powerful: the capacity to ask good questions. Curious leadership is not about having all the answers. It is about cultivating a culture where inquiry thrives, where uncertainty is not feared but embraced, and where learning is a shared endeavour.

The most effective leaders today are not heroic figures standing alone at the helm, but attentive learners who help others navigate complexity with clarity, purpose, and compassion. They understand that schools are living communities, not delivery systems, and that educational leadership is about listening as much as leading. Senge (1990) argued that learning organisations grow when their leaders create the conditions for continuous inquiry and reflective dialogue.

Curious leadership, then, is relational at its core. It begins not with strategy or compliance but with stance – a disposition of humility, openness, and deep respect for others. Curious leaders ask before they answer. They wonder before they act. They engage in dialogue not as a performance but as a path to deeper understanding. And they model the vulnerability required to say, 'I don't know yet, but let's find out together.'

This kind of leadership is not a luxury in today's educational landscape – it is a necessity. Schools are facing increasingly complex challenges: growing inequality, shifting student needs, community trauma, teacher burnout, and rapidly evolving expectations. Traditional, top-down leadership approaches often fall short in the face of such complexity. Fullan and Quinn (2016) contend that coherence emerges not from control but from purposeful, collaborative sense-making. Curious leaders facilitate that sense-making. They create the space where educators can surface tensions, share insights, and co-construct new directions.

In a suburban school facing declining enrolments, one principal began each leadership meeting with a single open-ended question: 'What are we learning about our students that we didn't know last week?' Over time, that question shifted the tone of decision-making – from reaction to reflection.

It prompted department heads to bring real insights to the table and helped reframe a climate of pressure into one of professional curiosity.

Curious leadership also requires courage. It involves challenging dominant narratives, asking uncomfortable questions, and protecting space for reflection even when external pressures demand quick fixes. In a system that often privileges certainty and speed, choosing to lead through inquiry can feel countercultural. But it is also profoundly liberating. It invites staff to move beyond compliance and rediscover their professional agency.

The inquiry compass: navigating leadership with curiosity

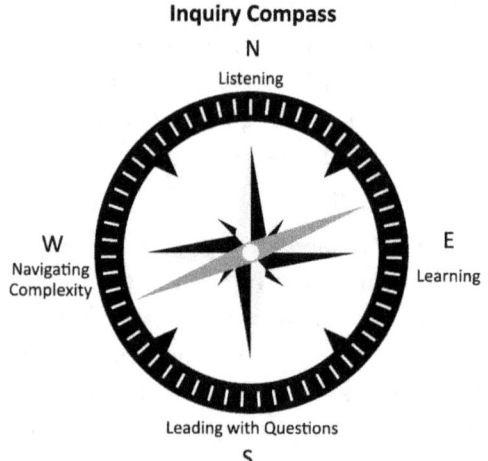

This visual frames curiosity as a leadership orientation rather than a fixed strategy. The four cardinal points represent practices that help leaders steer learning-centred schools:

- **North – listening:** deep, active attention to students, staff, families, and context
- **East – learning:** a commitment to personal and collective growth; modelling reflective practice
- **South – leading with questions:** creating psychological safety by posing rather than imposing; fostering open inquiry
- **West – navigating complexity:** holding ambiguity, resisting oversimplification, and adapting with care.

Rather than dictating a path, the compass enables leaders to **orient** themselves within complexity. It reminds us that in uncertain times leadership is less about having answers and more about creating the conditions for learning to emerge.

Throughout this chapter, we explore how curiosity reshapes the craft of leadership. We examine how inquiry, when led with integrity, can foster stronger teams, deeper learning, and more-inclusive school cultures. And we show how curiosity is not a distraction from leadership – it is its essence.

Having mapped the stance of curiosity, we now turn to how leaders can build the structures and rhythms to sustain it.

The architecture of curious leadership

Curious leadership doesn't begin with personality or charisma. It begins with intention. Leaders who want to embed curiosity in their schools must design for it – through structure, rhythm, and relationships. Without deliberate design, even the most insightful ideas remain isolated. What sustains inquiry over time is the way it becomes patterned into the daily life of a school.

Once a leader has begun building an environment where inquiry is possible, the next challenge is sustaining that culture through the everyday routines of the school.

This architecture includes:

- Time set aside for staff to reflect, question, and learn together
- Meetings designed for dialogue, not just information delivery
- Peer learning routines such as instructional rounds or collaborative inquiry groups
- Transparent processes that invite feedback and honour multiple perspectives.

In one school, leadership restructured weekly meetings using a simple three-question protocol: 'What are we noticing? What's going well? What do we want to learn more about?' This change replaced long agendas with genuine dialogue and shifted the culture from reporting to reflecting. The change was subtle but powerful – it gave staff permission to inquire.

This work is slow and subtle. It begins in staffrooms and planning meetings, in coaching conversations and corridor chats. It involves not just what is scheduled but how things feel. Do people feel safe to ask questions? Do they feel heard? Do they feel part of something bigger than their own classroom?

Relational trust is the foundation of improvement (Bryk et al., 2010). Without it, collaboration becomes compliance and reflection becomes ritual. Curious leaders invest in trust by making vulnerability visible. They share what they're learning. They acknowledge when they're unsure. They invite others into the process of meaning-making. This is not weakness – it's leadership with integrity.

The architecture of curiosity is also about permission. In many schools, the pressure to perform crowds out the time to think. Curious leaders push back against this. They defend learning time, not just for students but for staff. They advocate for policies and schedules that allow space for trial, error, and reflection. And they use their positional power not to control others but to create conditions in which others can grow.

Curious leaders often introduce routines that allow inquiry to become visible. These might include:

- Learning walks that focus on student thinking
- Data discussion protocols that value multiple interpretations
- Exit slips at meetings that ask, 'What are you still wondering about?'

According to Hargreaves and Fullan (2012), sustainable leadership depends on depth and breadth: depth of thinking, breadth of engagement. Curious leadership invites both. It attends to detail and context while drawing people into a shared sense of purpose. It replaces heroic leadership with distributed responsibility.

Ultimately, curious leadership is less about answers than about environments. It is about cultivating the trust, structure, and time required for thoughtful questions to surface and be pursued.

Curiosity as an ethical act

Curiosity in leadership is not just a technique – it is an ethical orientation. At its best, it is a form of moral attentiveness: a way of staying open to what we do not yet know, cannot fully see, or may prefer not to confront. To lead with curiosity is to lead with conscience.

Ethical leadership demands that we confront complexity honestly, not gloss over it with platitudes or efficiency. Curious leaders do not shy away from discomfort. They ask, 'What might we be missing?' and 'Whose voices are not yet heard?' These questions open space for inclusion and reflection, especially where habitual practice might exclude or overlook. Gardner et al. (2001) suggest that good work in education is not only technically excellent but also socially responsible and ethically guided.

Curiosity becomes an ethical force when directed toward equity and justice. In school communities marked by disadvantage, cultural marginalisation, or intergenerational trauma, curiosity offers a way in – an invitation to understand rather than to judge. Leaders who inquire into the lived experiences of students, staff, and families open the door to deeper empathy and more responsive practice.

Curious leaders ask hard questions about the systems they are part of:

- Why are some students consistently underrepresented in extension programs?
- How do our discipline policies affect students from different cultural or socioeconomic backgrounds?
- In what ways might our professional expectations marginalise part-time or early-career staff?
- How do our curriculum choices reflect or erase the identities of our learners?

These are not rhetorical questions. They are generative ones. They lead to action, not avoidance. They refuse the silence that often surrounds inequity. They surface the assumptions embedded in everyday routines and ask whether those routines align with the school's moral purpose.

This kind of curiosity requires moral courage. Ladson-Billings (1995) reminds us that equity work is not simply about supporting the underachieving – it is about rethinking the norms and structures that define success and belonging. Curious leadership resists the temptation to settle for technical solutions to adaptive challenges. It recognises that systems do not change unless people are willing to ask: What if we're wrong? What else could be true?

In one inner-urban school, a new principal noticed that behaviour data disproportionately targeted boys from refugee backgrounds. Rather than dismissing the numbers or rushing to retrain staff, she gathered teachers to reflect on their assumptions. Through shared inquiry, the staff re-examined classroom norms and uncovered a lack of cultural safety. They adapted their approach – and disciplinary referrals dropped dramatically. The shift wasn't procedural. It was ethical.

There is also an ethics of restraint in curious leadership. It resists the quick answer, the seductive certainty. It stays with questions longer. Good teaching and leadership, Palmer (1998) suggests, often involve holding paradox rather than resolving it – making space for tension and not rushing to closure.

Curious leaders lead ethically not only by asking questions but by changing the conditions under which questions can be asked. In doing so, they invest in building the school capital – trust, relational depth, collaborative capacity – that makes sustained inquiry possible. They redistribute voice and authority. They create systems where inquiry is not the privilege of a few, but the habit of the many. They elevate the importance of student agency, parent perspectives, and community engagement – not as token gestures, but as essential insights.

They also extend inquiry beyond the school gates, engaging families, students, and community partners as active participants in shared learning.

In doing so, they model what it means to be learners in a world that desperately needs thoughtful, just, and compassionate leadership.

Building cultures of inquiry

Leadership alone does not transform a school. What curious leaders do is spark, support, and sustain a culture of inquiry – a way of working that positions learning as everyone's business and questions as the engine of improvement.

Culture is not what we declare; it is what we repeatedly do. As Will Durant summarised Aristotle's thinking, 'We are what we repeatedly do. Excellence, then, is not an act but a habit' (Durant, 1926). In schools led by inquiry-minded leaders, collaboration, dialogue, and reflection are embedded in the rhythm of daily life. Teachers meet not just to plan content, but to explore student learning. Data becomes a prompt for exploration, not an instrument of control. Feedback is not a performance review – it is a conversation about practice. In this way, curiosity becomes woven into the fabric of leadership itself: not as an occasional flourish, but as a habit of mind and a shared professional stance.

This doesn't happen by accident. Professional learning communities flourish when teachers have regular, structured opportunities to inquire (Stoll & Louis, 2007). Curious leaders design those opportunities. They establish expectations that inquiry is part of practice, not an add-on. They understand that developing a strong trunk of school capital – intellectual, social, organisational, and even financial – creates the conditions in which curiosity can thrive.

They frame time for reflection as sacred, not optional. And they ensure that learning is distributed – not concentrated in the leadership team, but shared among all staff.

Curious leaders also protect the conditions in which inquiry can thrive:

- **Psychological safety:** where staff feel secure to speak candidly, raise doubts, and share early thinking without fear of judgment
- **Time and space:** where teams can meet regularly, explore student work, and reflect without being rushed
- **Trust and relational care:** where challenge is welcomed because it is grounded in mutual respect.

These conditions take time to build – but once established, they transform how a school thinks and acts. When inquiry becomes habitual, schools become more responsive, more resilient, and more capable of self-renewal.

In one primary school, a team of teachers worked with leadership to redesign their professional learning calendar. Instead of one-off workshops, they structured six-week inquiry cycles around shared dilemmas of practice. Each cycle included classroom experimentation, peer observation, evidence collection, and reflective discussion. The approach changed the way staff saw their own learning – less as compliance, more as growth.

Curious leaders understand that inquiry is not just something to promote; it is something to live. They model learning themselves – sharing their reading, inviting feedback on their leadership, participating in professional learning alongside staff, and openly grappling with dilemmas. This demystifies leadership and reinforces that growth is everyone's work.

Importantly, cultures of inquiry also spread beyond staff. Curious leaders create conditions where students, too, are part of the learning conversation. They support student voice initiatives, co-design learning experiences, and embed metacognition and reflection into classroom routines. When curiosity is systemic, it touches every layer of the school.

Performance and appraisal systems also shift in cultures of inquiry. In one secondary college, instructional coaching became central to teacher development, not as a tool for evaluation but as a space for shared learning. Staff used evidence of student work to set goals, reflect on progress, and adjust their practice. The language of judgment gave way to the language of improvement.

Curious leaders also encourage interdisciplinary inquiry – teachers working across subject areas to solve authentic problems. These collaborations not only deepen professional learning but often result in more engaging, relevant curriculum for students. Inquiry becomes a shared lens, not just an individual mindset.

Mitchell and Sackney (2011) emphasise that deep change happens when the school becomes a learning community in the fullest sense – where individual, interpersonal, and organisational learning are intertwined. Curious leaders hold this vision and build it daily, not through grand gestures, but through sustained attentiveness to how people learn together.

A culture of inquiry doesn't make a school perfect. But it does make it alive – capable of noticing, adjusting, and growing. In uncertain times, that is one of the most powerful assets a school can possess.

Yet building a culture of inquiry also demands courage from leaders themselves – a willingness to be vulnerable as learners in public view.

Leading with vulnerability: risks and rewards

To lead with curiosity is to lead with vulnerability. It requires letting go of the myth of certainty and stepping into spaces where answers are not pre-formed. Curious leaders choose honesty over image. They invite others to see not only their direction but their doubt.

This is not easy. Leadership is often constructed around control, confidence, and assurance. But inquiry requires a different kind of courage – the willingness to be seen as unfinished. Vulnerability is not a flaw in curious leadership. It is its foundation.

Brené Brown (2018) defines vulnerability as uncertainty, risk, and emotional exposure. In schools, this might look like a principal admitting when a new strategy isn't working, a middle leader asking for feedback from a resistant team, or a deputy choosing to share their own discomfort before facilitating a staff dialogue. These acts of vulnerability do not diminish leadership – they humanise it.

When leaders demonstrate vulnerability, they signal that learning is valued over performance. This encourages risk-taking, creativity, and honesty across the school. Staff are more likely to try new things, admit when they need support, and engage in authentic reflection. Trust is deepened. Energy is released.

This emotional openness does not mean abandoning boundaries or responsibility. It means leading with humanity. It means acknowledging that leadership is not about knowing more but about learning with curiosity, humility, and purpose.

And it means being strong enough to say, 'I don't know yet', without fearing loss of credibility.

Research on psychological safety (Edmondson, 2019) confirms that teams perform better when their leaders create conditions for candid dialogue and mutual respect. Vulnerability is not a risk to be managed – it is a practice to be embraced.

Curious leaders understand that emotional literacy is part of professional literacy. They attend to the emotional climate of their school. They recognise when fear, fatigue, or frustration are shaping behaviours – and they respond with empathy, not judgment. Vulnerability opens the door to compassion.

In many systems, however, vulnerability is discouraged by performance pressures. Public reporting, external reviews, and league tables can create environments where leaders feel they must present certainty at all costs. Curious leaders learn to hold that tension – to meet accountability requirements while still protecting space for honest learning. They model how to be open without being unprepared, transparent without being exposed.

In time, vulnerability becomes a cultural norm. People stop pretending. They show up fully. And this authenticity becomes the foundation for sustained improvement. Because schools don't thrive on performance alone – they thrive on trust, connection, and shared inquiry.

To lead with vulnerability is to lead with integrity. It is to model the very curiosity we hope to cultivate in others. And it is, perhaps, the most courageous step a leader can take.

The practice of leading through questions

The heart of curious leadership lies not in providing the quickest answers but in asking the most thoughtful questions. Questions are the compass of inquiry – they orient schools toward meaning, reflection, and possibility. They open space for conversation, surface assumptions, and unlock insight.

Curious leaders understand that questions are not the soft prelude to action; they are the work. They do not use them as rhetorical flourishes or to confirm their own views. They ask questions they genuinely don't yet know the answer to. And they do so consistently, until inquiry becomes embedded in the way the school thinks, plans, and responds.

Some of these questions are strategic:

- What are our students learning – and what are they really understanding?
- What patterns do we see in our data, and what might explain them?
- How do our current practices reflect our values and our context?

Some are cultural:

1. What kind of school are we becoming?
2. Who feels seen, heard, and valued here – and who might not?
3. How do we respond when things go wrong?

And some are deeply personal:

- What am I learning as a leader?
- What feedback am I hearing – and not hearing?
- How do I model the vulnerability and openness I ask of others?

These are not checklist questions. They are doorways. Asked with sincerity and followed with careful listening, they shape decisions, relationships, and learning environments. Wheatley (2002) describes great leadership as a willingness to start a conversation that matters – even when the path ahead is unclear.

In schools that have embraced curiosity, you can hear this shift in language. Staff talk about 'what we're noticing' and 'what we're learning', rather than 'what we've always done'. Teams frame their planning as cycles of inquiry, not delivery. Leaders ask, 'What surprised you this week?' at the end of staff meetings. These habits, small as they may seem, rewire the culture.

They move a school from reactive to reflective.

This is not just about tone. It is about mindset and structure. Curious leaders use protocols that support inquiry – learning rounds, case discussions, student work protocols, and reflective journals. They model disciplined inquiry over casual speculation. They protect time for questions that matter.

In a regional network of schools, leaders used the 'Spiral of Inquiry' (Timperley et al., 2014) to structure their collaboration. Each school team identified a focus area, scanned for evidence, developed hunches, explored new practices, and evaluated change. Rather than comparing test scores, they exchanged learning stories. The questions guided them, and the process created shared purpose.

And when questions do generate discomfort – as they often will – curious leaders stay present. They resist the urge to fix too quickly or move to resolution. They recognise that good questions unsettle before they clarify. They make space for the ambiguity, knowing that clarity will emerge through dialogue, not decree.

Over time, these habits shift what leadership means. It becomes less about performance and more about sense-making; less about control, more about contribution. The leader's role is not to drive the bus, but to nurture the conditions under which learning – deep, shared, lasting learning – can occur.

To close this chapter, perhaps the best metaphor is this: questions are the torchlight of leadership. They help us see what lies ahead, even if only partially. They cast light into the corners we may have overlooked. And they remind us, always, that the path forward is not paved by answers alone – but by the courage to keep asking.

Yet building a culture of inquiry also demands courage from leaders themselves – a willingness to be vulnerable as learners in public view.

From insight to action: leading for inquiry, equity, and change

Curious leadership is not a soft trait – it is a disciplined way of thinking, learning, and building trust. It models the vulnerability, inquiry, and shared purpose that sustain improvement over time. Leadership with curiosity invites others in and keeps the system alive to possibility.

For teachers:

- Adopt an 'inquiry first' stance in team discussions – ask, don't tell.
- Model curiosity with your students – share your own learning openly.
- Use simple protocols (learning walks, peer inquiry) to deepen team reflection.

For principals:

- Frame leadership questions for the year: What are we learning? What do we want to explore?
- Protect time in leadership meetings for open-ended dialogue, not just operational updates.
- Make visible your own uncertainties and learning – model leadership as inquiry.

For systems:

- Build leadership development programs around inquiry and adaptive capacity, not compliance.
- Reward leadership that fosters curiosity in others, not just performance outputs.
- Encourage networks of schools to explore collective inquiries into persistent challenges.

Curious leadership does not demand perfection – it demands presence, listening, and the courage to ask the questions that matter. That is how new futures are led into being.

The Curious Cat watches from the edge of the meeting room, whiskers twitching at the sound of an honest question. It recognises, with quiet approval, a leader brave enough to learn aloud.

Afterword: the quiet strength of inquiry

Curious leadership does not announce itself with slogans or dashboards. It reveals itself in the quiet, persistent commitment to asking better questions and listening more deeply – always anchored in moral purpose, and always supported by the school capital that enables a culture of trust and learning.

It is not about charisma, nor about control. It is about care – care for the work, for the people who do it, and for the students whose lives are shaped by it.

This chapter has shown that curiosity is not a soft skill, nor a luxury for when time permits. It is a discipline. A posture. A way of holding complexity without retreating into certainty. It requires courage to admit what we do not yet know, humility to learn from others, and clarity of purpose to stay the course.

In a world that often demands speed and certainty, curious leaders choose something else: to pause, to probe, and to grow. They hold space for reflection even when the clock is ticking. They trust in the collective wisdom of their teams. They understand that sustainable change cannot be driven by compliance alone – it must be cultivated through relationships, trust, and shared inquiry.

And perhaps most importantly, curious leaders do not lead alone. They build cultures in which everyone, from students to system executives, is invited into the work of wondering, discovering, and improving together. They lead not just for performance, but for possibility.

If leadership is, at its heart, an act of hope, then curiosity is its compass – pointing not toward easy answers, but toward deeper understanding.

But leadership alone is not enough. For curiosity to flourish at scale, it must travel through networks, policies, and system design. The next chapter explores what it takes to build such a curious system.

The Curious Cat lingers here, too – at the edge of the principal's office, curled beneath a leadership meeting table, perched beside the staff whiteboard. Watching. Listening. Waiting for the next good question.

CHAPTER 9

Unleashing the Curious System – Scaling Inquiry with Integrity

BIG IDEAS IN THIS CHAPTER

System change is not about replication – it's about enabling conditions. This chapter explores how curiosity can scale across schools and systems without becoming standardised.

Curious systems ask: What are we enabling, not just what are we delivering? This invites reflection on funding models, policy frameworks, network design, and leadership structures.

Sustainable reform needs coherence, not compliance. When systems are aligned around shared values – curiosity, equity, moral purpose – momentum builds from within.

Trust, not top-down control, is the real driver of large-scale improvement. Scaling curiosity requires a shift in mindset: from mandates to invitation, from metrics to meaning.

This chapter asks:

- What would a system look like if it were built to nurture curiosity, not just monitor performance?
- How might networks, policies, and partnerships come alive with inquiry?

'Systems resist change – but not forever.' – Margaret Wheatley

From fragmented innovation to collective inquiry

This flowchart illustrates how distributed inquiry, trust-based networks, and aligned policy mechanisms can move system reform beyond compliance and into scalable, curiosity-driven transformation.

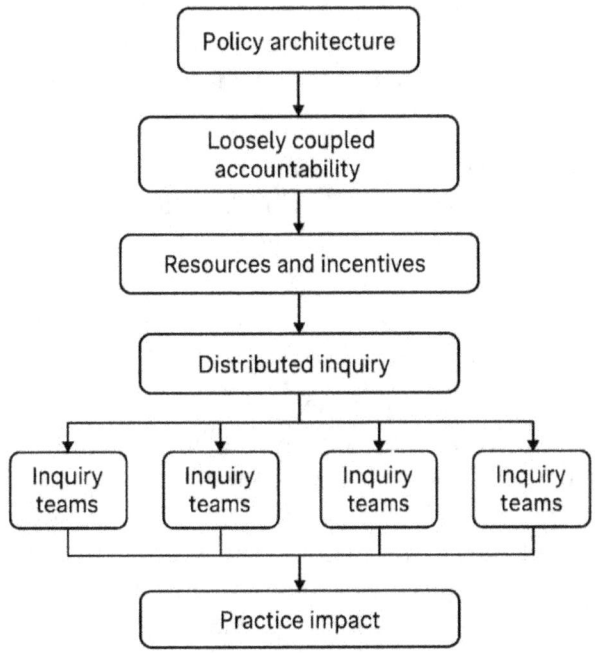

The story of educational reform is often told through the lens of isolated success – standout schools, exceptional leaders, or innovative pilot programs. These examples offer hope, but they also reveal a deeper problem: the chronic difficulty of scaling deep and lasting change across whole systems. Despite decades of reform, system-wide transformation remains elusive. Bright spots emerge, but the glow often fades before it spreads.

For every thriving school driven by inquiry and trust, there are others replicating templates without meaningful impact. For every dynamic principal modelling curiosity-led change, there are leaders overwhelmed by disconnected mandates, working in systems that reward compliance over reflection. This unevenness is not accidental. It is the result of how many systems are designed: to deliver, rather than to learn.

Reform efforts often falter not because the underlying ideas lack merit, but because the system is ill-equipped to absorb, interpret, and adapt them – a central insight from Michael Fullan (2011). Fragmentation becomes the default. Some schools innovate; others stagnate. Some teachers inquire; others are drowned by top-down directives. Reform becomes cyclical: a series of waves that crash without reshaping the shoreline.

What would it take to build a different kind of system – one where curiosity is not the exception but the norm; where change is not delivered to schools but co-constructed with them; where improvement is not episodic or leader-dependent but deeply embedded in the learning architecture of the system itself?

This chapter begins with that question. It contends that the future of school improvement depends not just on individual teacher capacity or school-level leadership but on a system-wide shift from delivery to inquiry. It suggests that educational systems, like schools and individuals, must themselves learn to learn. They must develop feedback-rich routines, collective reflective capacity, and a tolerance for complexity.

In many current systems, improvement is pursued through alignment: uniform curricula, assessment frameworks, inspection regimes. While coherence matters, alignment is often confused with control. The result is that schools are treated as delivery mechanisms, not dynamic communities. Innovation is boxed into programs. Curiosity is marginalised, particularly in schools serving disadvantaged communities where the stakes feel highest and the tolerance for deviation is lowest (Sahlberg, 2016).

And yet, there are examples that point toward a different possibility. In Ontario, Canada, system leaders focused on building instructional capacity and collaborative inquiry across all schools. Rather than impose rigid reform agendas, they invested in trust-building, peer learning, and moral purpose as drivers of change (Sharratt & Fullan, 2009). In Scotland, the Curriculum for Excellence was designed to provide a shared national direction while empowering schools to co-design rich, local learning experiences.

These examples show that deep change scales not through standardisation but through shared learning. Curiosity travels best not in mandates but in relationships. When systems act as learning ecosystems – distributing leadership, fostering reflection, and honouring the wisdom of schools – they become more coherent, not less.

This chapter explores what it takes to build such a system – a curious system; a system that protects the time, trust, and structures required for inquiry to thrive; a system that scales not by asking schools to copy each other but by helping them learn from and with one another; a system that does not chase silver bullets but builds slow, steady capacity for adaptive change.

To move beyond fragmentation, we need to shift the questions. Instead of asking 'Which schools are excelling?', we must ask: 'What are we learning across schools? What conditions allow inquiry to flourish? How do we build those conditions everywhere?'

The following sections explore these questions in practice – through system learning, network architecture, enabling policy, and the conditions for trust-based innovation. They invite us to see reform not as a product to deliver but as a process to steward.

How learning systems learn

Curiosity, like learning itself, needs structure. It does not flourish in a vacuum or under constant pressure. For inquiry to thrive at scale, systems must invest not only in people but in the architecture of learning – the formal and informal structures, routines, and rhythms that support professional dialogue, experimentation, and growth.

David Hopkins (2007) refers to this as the 'architecture of system reform' – a deliberate design that supports schools to pursue improvement as part of a connected, coherent system rather than in isolation. When systems build intentional structures that enable curiosity, they create the conditions for deeper, more coherent innovation. These structures allow ideas to move, grow, and evolve – not as top-down directives, but as shared inquiries. At the heart of such architecture lies school capital – the trust, expertise, organisational structures, and resources that enable schools to learn, not just implement. Without investing deliberately in these forms of capital, curiosity cannot scale sustainably.

A well-designed learning architecture includes multiple, interconnected layers:

- **Networks of schools engaged in collaborative inquiry**, where teachers and leaders co-develop knowledge, rather than merely share finished products. These networks encourage schools to bring real problems to the table and test solutions in context.

- **Coaching models** that develop internal expertise rather than external dependency. System leaders can seed capacity by training instructional coaches or inquiry facilitators who work across schools, helping teams to reflect on data, practice, and student thinking.
- **Protected time for professional learning**. Without time, even the best structures collapse. Learning architecture requires temporal architecture – making time for reflection, peer observation, data dialogue, and collaborative planning.
- **Shared platforms and tools** that invite openness. These might include protocols for sharing works-in-progress, learning stories, or teacher-led research. In curious systems, knowledge is not hoarded – it circulates.

These structural elements matter not because they ensure compliance but because they make learning **visible and repeatable**. Fullan and Quinn (2016) suggest that in complex systems coherence develops when the right drivers are aligned and actively shaping the work, and Lieberman and Miller (2004) remind us that learning is a social process. When the architecture of reform honours that truth, it produces collective efficacy. Schools become more confident in their ability to inquire, adapt, and improve – not because someone else told them what to do, but because they are engaged in learning that is meaningful, supported, and connected.

This architecture is not rigid. In fact, it must be adaptive. It should support diversity of approach within a coherent system narrative. What works in one community may not translate directly to another – but what can translate is the process of learning, reflection, and adaptation. Curious systems do not impose sameness. They coordinate, ensuring that local innovation contributes to a shared direction.

Consider a system that builds weekly inquiry time into its schools' schedules and backs it with trained peer coaches, cross-school learning teams, and a platform for sharing both promising practices and failed experiments. In such a system, curiosity is not a gamble – it is an expectation. The structure makes it safer to try, to reflect, to revise.

This kind of infrastructure signals that schools are not passive recipients of reform – they are active contributors. When systems are designed to capture and circulate what schools are learning, innovation spreads organically. A school's success becomes not a private achievement but a public contribution.

Over time, the architecture becomes a cultural asset. It builds muscle memory for learning – across schools, across roles, across cycles of reform. This is how a system begins to improve itself from the inside out.

In short, architecture matters – not because it enforces a vision, but because it enables learning. Curious systems do not rely on charismatic leadership or bursts of inspiration. They are designed – for trust, for reflection, and for sustained, shared inquiry.

Designing architecture for learning

Once architecture is in place, the deeper challenge begins: ensuring those structures don't just exist – they live. The most thoughtful designs are meaningless unless they are inhabited with intention, trust, and shared ownership. For learning to take root across a system, the formal must become cultural. And for that to happen, moral purpose must animate them. Without a clear ethical anchor – a commitment to equity, learning, and student wellbeing – inquiry risks becoming directionless or performative.

This means normalising inquiry across all layers of the system – not just in designated 'innovation zones' or occasional professional learning days, but in how problems are framed, how meetings are run, and how improvement is understood. A protocol for collaboration is helpful; a culture where curiosity is expected is transformational.

In curious systems, learning becomes part of the air people breathe:

- Principals use questions – not just data – to guide school reviews.
- Central offices model vulnerability by sharing missteps and lessons.
- Teachers see experimentation not as a risk but as a routine part of their practice.

When these mindsets are embedded, structures do more than support – they stretch. They enable systems to respond to new challenges without abandoning coherence. This is particularly vital in times of disruption, when rigid systems fracture. Adaptive learning cultures bend without breaking.

Critically, embedding learning also requires rethinking accountability. Instead of asking, 'Did you follow the program?' systems can ask, 'What have you learned? What changed as a result? What might others learn from this?' These questions shift the improvement narrative from control to contribution.

Resilient systems don't just create the conditions for learning – they steward them. They invest not only in architecture, but in the dispositions and relationships that allow that architecture to be used with insight, creativity, and purpose. Structure may be the scaffolding – but culture is the climb.

But architecture alone is not enough. For ideas to spread and curiosity to thrive across diverse contexts, relationships matter. Networks are the critical enablers of this spread.

Networks as engines of spread

If curiosity is to scale, it cannot travel alone. It needs a carrier. In education systems, the most effective carriers of innovation are **networks** – not bureaucratic clusters or compliance-based groupings, but intentional, trust-rich partnerships rooted in shared learning.

For too long, the spread of educational improvement has been based on replication: copying a successful model, rolling it out across sites, and expecting similar results. This approach misunderstands how change works. Context matters. Relationships matter. Interpretation matters. Networks offer a different theory of spread – not replication, but diffusion through inquiry.

In effective networks, schools don't just exchange templates. They share puzzles. They co-investigate problems of practice. They visit each other's classrooms not to evaluate but to understand. The flow of learning moves laterally, not just vertically – from school to school, teacher to teacher – building trust, shared purpose, and deeper insight.

Hargreaves and Ainscow (2015) describe networks as 'the social capital of system improvement'. They create the connective tissue that enables ideas to move, adapt, and stick. But this only happens when the network itself is treated as a learning entity – not a delivery mechanism. Strong networks:

- Identify shared questions of practice rather than enforce shared solutions
- Create opportunities for joint practice development, not just show-and-tell
- Use evidence to prompt reflection, not competition
- Define progress collectively, grounded in local context and moral purpose.

Coburn (2003) distinguishes between surface-level adoption of reforms and deeper spread characterised by 'depth, sustainability, and ownership'. Networks, when properly supported, foster the latter. They enable teachers and leaders to make meaning of reform in ways that are contextually relevant and pedagogically sound.

An example of this is the Learning Frontiers initiative in Australia, developed by the Australian Institute for Teaching and School Leadership (AITSL) in collaboration with the UK-based Innovation Unit. The project brought together clusters of schools to co-design learning practices that fostered student engagement and agency. Rather than disseminating pre-packaged solutions, Learning Frontiers provided a structured framework for schools to engage in design thinking, collective inquiry, and peer exchange. Its core approach centred on professional trust and co-creation, empowering educators to design and iterate practices in response to their own contexts. The lasting impact was not only the strategies that emerged, but the enduring habits of collaboration, reflection, and practitioner-led innovation that it cultivated across the network.

Similarly, Networked Improvement Communities (NICs), as described by Bryk et al. (2015), bring an engineering mindset to education networks – emphasising continuous improvement, disciplined inquiry, and shared measurement. These networks don't chase innovation for its own sake. They focus on specific outcomes, use cycles of inquiry to test changes, and share learning openly.

But these benefits are not automatic. Networks must be nurtured. They require time, facilitation, and resourcing. System leaders must prioritise their health – not as a 'nice to have', but as a strategic investment in capacity-building. Without sustained support, networks can collapse under logistical pressures or revert to superficial information-sharing.

Crucially, networks also need psychological safety. Edmondson (2019) suggests that environments where people feel safe to speak up, admit failure, and ask questions are more likely to learn and innovate. In well-functioning networks, schools feel safe to be honest. They share not just successes but struggles. This vulnerability, shared within a trusted circle, becomes a wellspring of growth.

Networks also allow systems to scale nuance. Rather than forcing all schools to adopt the same strategies, networks allow different sites to adapt ideas in ways that make sense for their learners. This balances coherence with autonomy. It builds what Stoll et al. (2006) call 'connected professionalism' – the sense that educators are part of something larger, without losing their agency or voice.

When seen this way, networks are not peripheral. They are central to the system's capacity to learn. They reduce duplication, amplify insight, and create momentum. Innovation spreads not because it is mandated but because people trust each other enough to explore uncertainty together.

Over time, networks become the carriers of culture. They encode new norms – sharing, questioning, reflecting – and reinforce the habits of inquiry. They enable system learning not through scale-up but through scale-deep. The spread is slower – but stickier, richer, and more sustainable.

In a curious system, networks are not a tactic. They are the terrain. They make the invisible pathways of professional learning visible and walkable. And in doing so, they allow curiosity to move – not just within schools but between them.

The power of networks lies in their capacity to spread curiosity through trust and shared inquiry – not through replication. Yet in many systems, initial reluctance runs deep. Schools often hesitate to engage in improvement initiatives for fear of being seen as needing help, or as losing professional autonomy. One example from Victoria illustrates how a carefully designed, trust-based approach helped overcome this resistance and transformed learning culture across an entire region.

> ### Vignette: Building a curious system in Victoria
>
> *A story of how curiosity scaled through networks, trust, and system design.*
>
> In Victoria's northern metropolitan region, a voluntary school improvement initiative began with a simple but provocative framing: Literate, Numerate and Curious. The goal was not to mandate improvement strategies, but to invite schools to explore how curiosity – alongside foundational capabilities – could drive deeper learning and professional growth.
>
> At the time, involvement in school improvement initiatives was not a sought-after option. In fact, there was a degree of stigma attached. 'Good' schools – those seen as high-performing – often kept their distance from such programs, wary of being perceived as needing help. Many school leaders had seen waves of disconnected reforms come and go, leaving staff weary and sceptical. The initial reluctance was real. But this initiative was different. Its design appealed to something deeper: to the moral purpose of school leaders and teachers, to their inherent desire for collegiality, and to the likelihood that the work would enhance both student outcomes and teacher satisfaction.

Schools opted in voluntarily. System leaders worked alongside Professor David Hopkins and regional staff to design an approach grounded in trust and inquiry. The model offered professional learning with the principal present, peer coaching with release time, and co-investment funding to support sustained reflection and action.

The impact surprised even the organisers. In the first year, 60 schools joined. The following year, 60 more came on board. Within three years, all 200 schools in the region had engaged with the work. Importantly, curiosity did not travel through mandates; it travelled through networks. As teachers and leaders shared questions, insights, and emerging practices across schools, a genuine learning culture began to take root.

Outcomes followed. Student engagement rose. Literacy and numeracy gains were evident. Staff morale improved. Relationships with families strengthened. And a renewed sense of professional pride spread across the region – not because compliance had increased, but because curiosity had been protected and empowered.

The experience demonstrated a key lesson: when system leaders trust schools as learning communities, and when networks are designed to foster inquiry rather than enforce compliance, curiosity can scale – not as a program, but as a culture.

The role of policy in curious systems

Policy is not neutral. It signals what matters, who matters, and what is safe to explore. In a curious system, policy is not just a lever of control – it becomes a signal of trust, clarity, and direction. Done well, policy can create the psychological and structural space for schools to inquire, adapt, and innovate.

Unfortunately, policy too often sends the opposite signal. Schools experience reform as a cascade of mandates – frequent, fragmented, and often disconnected from practice. Policymaking becomes reactive, driven by headlines, electoral cycles, or political optics rather than by sustained engagement with educators and evidence. This breeds cynicism and narrows the space for curiosity, especially in disadvantaged settings where fear of failure is amplified.

In contrast, curious systems treat policy as part of the learning architecture. Policies are not imposed upon schools but co-constructed with them. They are crafted through consultation, iterative testing, and shared reflection. The policy-making process itself models inquiry: listening, adjusting, and refining over time.

Consider the recommendations from the Gonski 2.0 Review (Gonski et al., 2018), which emphasised growth, deep learning, and student agency. While implementation has been uneven, the intent was clear: to shift policy from content coverage to capability development, and to enable schools to design context-responsive approaches. This represents a move from prescription to direction – an essential distinction in curious systems.

Curious policies:

- Provide a clear moral and educational purpose without prescribing a narrow path
- Build in flexibility, allowing for local adaptation and innovation
- Include feedback mechanisms, so that insights from practice inform policy evolution
- Value qualitative data – such as narrative evidence of student growth – alongside metrics
- Signal that learning is the goal, not just compliance.

In Scotland's *Curriculum for Excellence*, policy explicitly values teacher autonomy, student voice, and cross-disciplinary capability. The curriculum framework offers broad guidance on what young people should learn, but leaves significant room for co-design at the school level. This balance of structure and freedom supports curiosity both in classrooms and in leadership practice (Priestley & Biesta, 2013).

Policy must also attend to conditions, not just outcomes. A funding model, for example, that incentivises competition and performance metrics may stifle collaboration and inquiry. In contrast, policies that fund teacher release time, coaching, and cross-school networks enable the work of learning to unfold.

Ladwig and Luke (2014) argue that policy, when developed with a focus on justice and inclusion, becomes a vehicle for ethical reform. In curious systems, this means that policies must not only allow innovation, but protect it – particularly in schools serving vulnerable populations, where the margin for error can feel unforgiving.

Ultimately, the best policies do not control – they invite. They extend an open hand to educators and say: *You are trusted. You are valued. You are capable of learning and leading.* This is the kind of signal that awakens system-wide inquiry.

Yet even with supportive policies, curiosity will only thrive if the day-to-day conditions in schools and systems make it safe, possible, and expected. These conditions are what we turn to next.

Creating the conditions for curiosity at scale

Scaling inquiry across a system is not about enforcing curiosity. It is about enabling it. This distinction matters. Curious systems do not mandate mindset shifts or prescribe reflective practice – they build the conditions that make inquiry possible, desirable, and sustainable.

These conditions are not checkboxes. They are cultural and structural dispositions embedded across roles and layers. When they are present, schools feel safe to think, leaders feel supported to listen, and systems become more coherent – not through control, but through shared learning.

Psychological safety

Curiosity requires vulnerability. Asking genuine questions – especially in the presence of peers or supervisors – can feel risky. Educators need to feel safe to say, 'I don't know' or 'This didn't work.' Without that safety, inquiry is stifled and reflection becomes performative.

Amy Edmondson's (2019) research on psychological safety shows that high-performing teams are those in which members feel safe to speak up, make mistakes, and challenge norms. In education, this applies to classrooms, staffrooms, and central offices alike. Curious systems foster a culture where uncertainty is not punished but welcomed as a catalyst for learning.

Time for thought

In Victoria, Australia, schools involved in system-wide peer-coaching initiatives found that the most significant barrier was not will – but time. When time was protected and coaching embedded into school routines, professional dialogue flourished. Teachers moved from 'How do I cover content?' to 'What's really happening in my students' thinking?' – a shift only made possible by dedicated time to reflect and explore.

Trust in the field

Curious systems are built on trust – not the absence of accountability, but the presence of respect. Central leaders in these systems assume that teachers want to grow, that principals know their communities, and that schools can lead improvement when given the right support.

This trust must be reciprocal. Schools also need to trust that central offices will listen, adapt, and learn alongside them. This doesn't mean an anything-goes approach – it means enabling responsibility rather than enforcing compliance.

Bryk et al. (2010) found that relational trust was a key driver of sustained improvement across diverse Chicago schools. It wasn't technical fixes that improved student learning – it was the depth and strength of relationships.

Slow thinking leadership

Systems that scale curiosity don't just change policies – they change how leaders behave. Curious leaders practise what Daniel Kahneman (2011) calls 'slow thinking': deliberate, reflective, and open to challenge. They resist premature answers and instead model inquiry.

These leaders ask before they direct. They listen before they act. They design meetings that begin with questions, not checklists. And they protect the learning of others as fiercely as they pursue their own. This kind of leadership sends a powerful signal: *Thinking is valued here.*

Purpose as anchor

Curiosity without direction drifts. That is why moral purpose must anchor systems-level inquiry, and why school capital – the professional trust, expertise, and relational depth that sustain learning cultures – must be deliberately cultivated. Curious systems are not built on curiosity alone. They rest on the deep roots of moral purpose and the strong trunk of school capital. Together, these provide coherence and resilience as curiosity spreads.

Curious systems are anchored by moral purpose. They are clear about what matters – equity, learning, wellbeing – and align their inquiries around these aims. This clarity gives people permission to explore *how* to improve, while remaining grounded in *why* it matters.

Palmer (1998) writes that 'good teaching cannot be reduced to technique; good teaching comes from the identity and integrity of the teacher'. Systems, too, must act with integrity – ensuring that their pursuit of innovation does not disconnect from the students and communities they serve.

When these conditions are present, inquiry becomes not just possible, but expected. It moves beyond isolated projects or enthusiastic individuals. It becomes a systemic norm – not because people are told to be curious, but because the environment makes curiosity feel natural, supported, and safe.

This is what enables curiosity to travel – not as a program, but as a way of being.

Curiosity without coherence fails

Curiosity is powerful – but without coherence, it falters. Systems that try to scale inquiry by simply encouraging experimentation or promoting innovation in isolated pockets often find that energy dissipates: initiatives fragment, schools move in different directions, trust frays, innovation stalls.

This is the paradox of curiosity at scale: too little structure, and inquiry becomes chaotic; too much, and it becomes performative. The answer is not uniformity, but coherence – a shared sense of purpose, direction, and language that enables diverse practices to connect and evolve.

Michael Fullan and Joanne Quinn (2016) define coherence as the 'shared depth of understanding about the purpose and nature of the work'. It is not imposed alignment. It is internal clarity. When systems achieve coherence, they don't all do the same thing – but they know *why* they're doing it, and how their actions contribute to broader learning and improvement.

In a curious system, coherence is built not through checklists but through:

- **Shared values:** A system-wide commitment to equity, learning, and the moral purpose of education.
- **Common language:** Terms like 'inquiry', 'reflection', and 'collaboration' mean the same things across schools and roles.
- **Anchoring metaphors:** Frameworks like the School Improvement Tree can provide visual, flexible coherence – offering shared conceptual ground without rigid prescription.
- **Structures for shared learning:** Cross-school dialogues, collaborative planning protocols, and learning sprints provide rhythm and focus.

Without coherence, curiosity can become a drain. Teachers and leaders are pulled in competing directions. Professional learning becomes fragmented. The system loses its capacity to reflect because it is chasing too many goals with too little connection. But with coherence, curiosity becomes more than energy – it becomes momentum. Schools see themselves as part of a larger story. Local innovation feeds system-wide learning. Improvement becomes cumulative rather than episodic.

Trust-based, curiosity-led improvement is not a utopian ideal; it can take hold even in highly challenged, policy-constrained contexts – if the system is willing to let go of tight control and allow inquiry to flourish. One powerful example comes from the Broadmeadows area in Melbourne's north, where a cluster of schools broke through years of compliance fatigue by re-centring curiosity and trust at the heart of their improvement work.

Vignette: Taking the foot off the accelerator – Trust and curiosity in Broadmeadows

A story of how leadership trust unlocked inquiry and professional growth across a struggling school community.

This example comes from schools in the Broadmeadows area prior to the regeneration project. These schools had long struggled under waves of compliance-driven, frequently disconnected reform. On one side of the railway line, schools were working to implement one set of improvement initiatives; on the other side, an entirely different suite of programs was in place. The schools groaned under the weight of 'programmitis', as well-intentioned bureaucratic efforts repeatedly brought in external experts to address persistent underperformance.

Leadership teams, weary of this cycle of initiative churn, leapt at the opportunity to join a trust-based, curiosity-led professional learning model, centred on staff-designed inquiry cycles. The model had been proposed by the newly installed regional leadership team. While some system leaders remained sceptical, the experiment proceeded under close observation.

Rather than mandating programs, the schools co-created shared inquiry questions around student engagement and literacy growth. Teachers undertook action research in their own classrooms, shared their learning through cross-school networks, and incorporated student voice into the redesign of learning experiences.

> The results soon surprised even the central office. Not only did student outcomes begin to improve, but student and parent engagement, teacher morale, and staff retention strengthened markedly. As an assistant regional director observed: 'When we took our foot off the compliance accelerator and made space for trust and curiosity, the system started learning again.'

This experience reinforced a core lesson for system leaders: trust and curiosity are not soft options. They are powerful enablers of adaptive improvement – especially in contexts where top-down reform has repeatedly failed. When systems shift from enforcing compliance to enabling inquiry, they don't just free schools to improve; they begin to build the adaptive capacity of the system itself.

Timperley, Kaser, and Halbert (2014) describe this as the capacity to inquire: not freeform exploration, but rigorous, purpose-driven learning that is locally adapted and centrally supported. This requires deliberate design. Systems must provide enough structure to guide, but enough space to grow.

The School Improvement Tree offers one example of this kind of coherence. With moral purpose as the root, school capital as the trunk, and curiosity as the canopy representing a range of student and system outcomes, the model allows educators to see how their context-specific actions connect to a shared theory of change. It supports diversity while holding a common frame – exactly what a curious system needs.

Ultimately, coherence is not about closing possibilities – it's about making inquiry *stick*. It is the connective tissue that links reflection to impact, experimentation to purpose, and local change to collective transformation.

Yet even with supportive policies, curiosity will only thrive if the day-to-day conditions in schools and systems make it safe, possible, and expected. These conditions are what we turn to next.

Looking ahead

A curious system is never finished.

Unlike programmatic reform or top-down policy rollouts, the work of scaling inquiry is inherently unfinished. It unfolds over time, through relationships, reflection, and iteration. It does not move in straight lines, nor does it follow fixed timelines. It deepens, shifts, and renews itself – if the conditions are right.

This chapter has offered a view of what such a system could look like: one that learns from itself, designs infrastructure for professional reflection, builds networks that connect rather than constrain, crafts policies that invite rather than dictate, and embeds conditions that support not only the *what* of schooling, but the *how* and *why*. It is a system that scales not just programs, but possibility.

Yet even the most thoughtfully designed system will face challenges. Leaders change. Funding dries up. Political winds shift. Fatigue sets in. The question is not whether disruption will come – it will. The real question is whether the system has built the adaptive capacity to keep learning in spite of, and sometimes because of, those disruptions.

This is the heart of the next chapter.

Where Chapter 9 has focused on structures, partnerships, and levers of system-level transformation, Chapter 10 turns inward and forward. It explores what sustains this work over time – what allows curiosity to outlast an initiative, to persist through leadership turnover, to survive in schools that have seen reform come and go. It asks: 'What endures? How do we build not just learning systems, but learning cultures that are robust enough to weather complexity without losing their soul?'

In other words, Chapter 10 is about **stewardship** – about the quiet, sustained work of protecting and cultivating curiosity – not just as a spark of reform, but as the lifeblood of schools and systems.

And so, as this chapter closes, the Curious Cat takes a step back – not into retreat, but into the wider system. It observes the connections forming between schools. It notices the questions being asked in policy circles. It senses the old habits loosening. The system is beginning to learn.

Slowly, perhaps. Unevenly, certainly. But unmistakably.

From insight to action: scaling inquiry with integrity

Curiosity cannot remain the property of individual classrooms or schools – it must scale across networks and systems to enable collective learning and sustained reform. Curious systems foster the conditions in which curiosity becomes a force for equity, innovation, and shared purpose.

For teachers:

- Participate in cross-school networks with an inquiry stance – what are others learning that you can explore?
- Share your own questions and insights beyond your immediate team or school – be an agent of curiosity across the system.
- Use data collaboratively – as a starting point for exploration, not simply for comparison or ranking.

For principals:

- Build partnerships with other schools based on shared inquiry – not competition.
- Invite system leaders to walk alongside your school's inquiry work – transparency builds trust and spreads learning.
- Design school improvement plans as dynamic documents – living inquiries rather than static targets.

For systems:

- Design accountability frameworks that reward inquiry and reflection as much as short-term results.
- Enable networked learning – create space, funding, and permission for cross-school inquiry and experimentation.
- Protect curiosity in system language and culture – leaders model whether curiosity is safe or suppressed.

A curious system is not one where every school does the same thing – it is one where every school learns, together, in ways that reflect their students, their communities, and their shared future.

And the Cat, ever observant, now prowls the edges of the system. It sees connections forming, networks sparking, old habits loosening. The system is learning. Slowly, perhaps – but unmistakably.

Afterword: scaling with integrity

The phrase 'system reform' too often conjures images of grand plans, flowcharts, and top-down strategies. But the most transformative systems are not those that move the fastest or sound the most ambitious. They are those that learn – with humility, with patience, and with integrity.

This chapter has challenged the idea that scaling requires replication. It has shown that systems grow not by imposing blueprints but by cultivating cultures – of trust, reflection, and shared purpose. Scaling inquiry is not about creating carbon copies of high-performing schools. It is about enabling *each* school to become a place of thoughtful learning, in its own context and community.

To do this, systems must attend as much to the *how* as to the *what*. Structures matter, but only if they are animated by curiosity and sustained by care. Policy matters, but only when it invites rather than dictates. Networks matter, but only when they are anchored in shared moral purpose and grounded in the realities of everyday practice. They also rely on school capital – the conditions that allow inquiry to be enacted meaningfully, not just imagined. Without strong professional relationships, time for reflection, and organisational trust, curiosity withers.

The central argument of this chapter is simple but radical: that curiosity can scale – not as a program, but as a way of being. When the right conditions are in place, inquiry spreads. When systems honour the intelligence of the field, trust deepens. And when learning is protected at every level, change becomes something we grow into – not something we chase.

Scaling with integrity means asking, again and again: Are we learning, or are we delivering? Are we building coherence, or just compliance? Are we stewarding curiosity – or stifling it?

These are questions not just for systems, but for the people who shape them.

That is how transformation begins. Quietly. Collectively. And with curiosity at the core.

The final chapter turns to the long view: how we can sustain curiosity-led improvement over time, through changes in leadership, policy, and culture – and how we can keep the system itself learning.

And so, the Curious Cat takes one last glance before stepping into the shadows of the system – watching for signs that the culture is shifting, that dialogue is deepening, that inquiry is travelling. Not because someone mandated it, but because people believe in it.

CHAPTER 10

The Cat's Next Step – Sustaining a Movement Over Time

BIG IDEAS IN THIS CHAPTER

Movements endure when they are rooted in purpose, not personality. This final chapter explores what it takes to keep curiosity alive – not just as an idea, but as a cultural rhythm.

Sustainability requires more than strategy – it calls for stewardship. The work continues through rituals, stories, shared language, and leadership that honours both continuity and change.

Curiosity doesn't end with a model – it evolves with context. The chapter reflects on how to stay responsive, adaptive, and hopeful even when the spotlight fades.

This is not about legacy – it's about regeneration. What practices, values, and relationships will ensure the work doesn't just last, but deepens over time?

This chapter asks:

- What outlasts the project, the initiative, the leader?
- How can we pass on the flame of curiosity – quietly, consistently, and courageously?

'There is a crack in everything, that's how the light gets in.'
– Leonard Cohen

Beyond the spark

Curiosity, we've seen throughout this book, is a powerful catalyst. It stirs the stagnant, unsettles the certain, and reawakens learning – not just in students, but in teachers, leaders, and entire systems. It reminds us that learning is not a linear march from known to unknown, but a dance with possibility. And in schools where curiosity gains traction, something shifts. Conversations change. Classrooms open up. Assumptions loosen. Energy returns.

But the challenge for schools is not only to spark curiosity – it's to sustain it. The real work begins once the initial flame has caught. For curiosity to become a way of working rather than a one-off event, it must outlast enthusiasm. It must survive leadership transitions, navigate policy churn, and persist through periods of fatigue and uncertainty. Nurturing curiosity over time is not about a singular charismatic leader or a glossy new initiative. It is about embedding inquiry into the very fabric of a school's culture.

Many reform efforts falter because they mistake change for improvement. Michael Fullan (2011) has argued that true change is not achieved by simply layering new programs on top of old structures, but by shifting the underlying norms and beliefs that govern practice. Curiosity, therefore, cannot remain an 'add-on' to the real work – it *is* the work. And when inquiry is woven into daily routines, expectations, and conversations, it becomes both a driver of change and a protector against stasis.

However, sustaining curiosity over time is no small task. It competes with powerful forces: performance pressures, rigid accountability systems, and initiative fatigue. Teachers are often caught in a tension between compliance and creativity, between scripted curriculum delivery and the human complexity of student learning. In such conditions, curiosity is not fragile, but it is vulnerable. Without intentional structures and shared values to protect it, curiosity can quickly become performative – or abandoned altogether (Hargreaves & Shirley, 2009).

This is why the final frontier of curiosity is not inspiration, but infrastructure. The question is not just 'How do we start?' but 'How do we keep going?'

What enables a school to protect and extend its curiosity when enthusiasm wanes, when complexity mounts, and when results are slow to materialise?

The answer lies in the soil, not the seed. Cultivating sustainable curiosity requires attention to the conditions that support it: the culture of the school, the nature of its leadership, the design of its systems, and the strength of its purpose. When these are aligned, curiosity can take root and flourish – not just in one classroom or during one project, but across time and across the school community.

Schools that manage to sustain inquiry often do so quietly. They don't always attract headlines or accolades. But beneath the surface, something profound is happening: learning is becoming collective, trust is being built, and a culture of shared responsibility is emerging. These are the schools that resist fads, not through cynicism but through discernment. They know who they are, what they value, and why it matters. And in that clarity, they make room for curiosity to become more than a spark. It becomes a source of strength.

As we move into the final reflections of this book, we turn to the elements that allow curiosity not just to ignite but to endure. The journey from spark to sustainability depends not on programs but on people – and on the cultures, leadership, systems, and purposes they co-create.

Culture that holds

In schools where curiosity becomes part of daily life, culture comes first – and that culture rests on strong school capital: the trust, relationships, professional expertise, and organisational rhythms that make learning sustainable.

Too often, educational reform begins with the technical – new initiatives, frameworks, or programs – without attending to the deeper patterns of how people relate, how decisions are made, and how learning is valued. Yet as Fullan (2006) reminds us – echoing Peter Drucker – 'culture eats strategy for breakfast'. This is especially true for curiosity. A school can declare its commitment to inquiry, but if its culture prizes certainty over exploration, or compliance over reflection, curiosity will wither.

Curious schools are not built overnight. They are cultivated, season by season, through the repeated, relational work of dialogue, trust, and shared risk-taking. In these schools, inquiry is not reserved for staff meetings or project days. It is part of the daily rhythm. It shows up in how teachers speak with one another, how students are encouraged to question, how leaders listen, and how families are engaged.

These are schools where a planning meeting might begin not with 'What's our target?' but 'What are we noticing?' - where curiosity frames the conversation, not just the outcomes. They protect space for collective reflection, resisting the pressure to rush from data to decision. They treat feedback as fuel, not failure. And crucially, they honour the discomfort that often comes with learning - seeing vulnerability not as a weakness but as a necessary companion to growth.

This cultural orientation is not superficial. It is sustained over time and across leadership transitions. It lives in both the formal structures and informal norms - the questions people ask, the silences they allow, and the stories they share. As Bryk et al. (2010) observed in their research on successful schools in Chicago, sustained improvement is less about innovation and more about organisational learning. That learning, they found, was built on a bedrock of relational trust.

Trust is the oxygen of a curious culture. It allows teachers to take risks without fear of humiliation, to admit when they don't know, and to seek help when they need it. It empowers leaders to say, 'Let's find out together', instead of pretending to have all the answers. And it enables students to see school not as a performance arena but as a place of discovery.

One of the key features of these cultures is their consistency. They don't rely on a singular charismatic leader or an occasional burst of innovation. Rather, they develop what Bryk and colleagues called 'a culture of continuous improvement' - a steady, predictable commitment to learning that becomes embedded in the DNA of the school. It's not that these schools never falter; it's that they return again and again to inquiry as a way of working.

This aligns with Tyack and Tobin's (1994) influential notion of the 'grammar of schooling' - the deep, often unspoken routines and expectations that shape school life. While the concept was introduced more than three decades ago, it remains one of the most useful ways to understand why surface-level reforms so often falter: the underlying grammar resists change. Yet in truly curious schools, the grammar itself begins to shift - not through mandate, but through repeated patterns of practice. Reflection becomes normal. Uncertainty becomes acceptable. Dialogue becomes central. Over time, these habits no longer require permission; they become embedded in how the community works. Just as Aristotle suggested that excellence is forged through repetition, so too is a culture of inquiry sustained by what educators do, together, day after day.

And yet, culture alone is not enough. That's why the most sustained and adaptive cultures are also well-resourced. Without supportive structures – time for collaboration, routines for feedback, opportunities for professional learning – culture can become aspiration rather than action. That's why the most enduring cultures are also well-resourced – not necessarily in terms of money, but in terms of attention. Leaders in these schools devote real time to building relationships, designing purposeful meetings, and recognising growth. They don't just talk about curiosity – they make space for it.

Consider the simple act of protecting time. In one school I worked with, the principal restructured timetables to ensure that every teacher had an hour of collaborative planning each week with their year-level team. There was no set agenda – just a shared commitment to explore what was working, what wasn't, and what they were noticing in their students. Over time, this small structural shift transformed the culture. Inquiry became normal. Professional dialogue deepened. And most importantly, student learning improved – not because of a single program, but because the school had built the cultural muscle to keep learning.

This is what I mean by a *culture that holds*. Such a culture doesn't just tolerate inquiry, but expects it, treating questioning as a sign of care rather than a threat. It survives changes in leadership because it belongs to the community – not just the principal or the leadership team, but the staff, the students, and the families who co-create it.

In these schools, culture keeps curiosity alive even when no one is watching. It holds fast when external pressures mount. It carries the learning forward – quietly, steadily, and with a sense of shared commitment that endures beyond any single moment or mandate.

Leadership that listens

If culture keeps curiosity alive, then leadership creates the conditions in which it can flourish: not with grand visions or rigid plans, but with attentiveness – with a way of leading that listens before it speaks.

Curious schools are led by curious leaders. These are not always the loudest voices in the room. They are often the ones asking the quiet questions: *What are we noticing? What's changing? What do we need to understand before we act?* They don't see their role as telling others what to do, but as creating the space in which others can learn. As Palmer (1998) notes, good leaders 'create and protect spaces for the human spirit to grow'.

Curious leadership depends not only on personal stance, but on the health of the school's social and intellectual capital. Leaders invest in trust and professional growth as deliberately as they invest in vision. Without these forms of capital, curiosity struggles to take root beyond the individual teacher or classroom. Such leadership requires humility. It means relinquishing the illusion of control and embracing the complexity of school life. It means recognising that good questions often matter more than quick answers. In curious schools, leaders model inquiry. They are visible not just in decision-making but in learning – joining professional dialogues, participating in lesson studies, reflecting publicly on their own practice.

This isn't a soft form of leadership. It's rigorous in its intentionality. Leaders who foster curiosity do not simply 'step back'; they design processes and structures that keep learning at the centre. They are architects of rhythm and coherence. They understand that curiosity doesn't just happen – it must be invited, protected, and cultivated.

One of the most powerful ways they do this is by distributing leadership. In many schools, leadership is still overly concentrated – dependent on a single principal to drive change, maintain focus, and hold the cultural line. But sustainability depends on leadership that is shared. As Spillane (2006) argues, distributed leadership is not about giving people more to do; it's about changing how leadership is understood and enacted.

In curious schools, inquiry lives not just in the principal's office, but in middle-leader meetings, peer-coaching relationships, team planning sessions, and classroom conversations. It flows through the system horizontally, not just vertically. Teachers are invited into leadership roles – not as token participants, but as co-designers of change. This aligns with Lieberman and Miller's (2004) research, which found that schools thrive when teachers are positioned as leaders of learning, not just implementers of it.

Importantly, leadership for curiosity is often invisible. It happens in the background – setting the tone, asking the second question, ensuring the structures are in place for reflection to occur. It is leadership that tunes in, rather than tunes out; that notices tension and holds space for discomfort;

that protects time for professional inquiry, even when pressure mounts to move quickly.

Consider a school where the leadership team sets aside 15 minutes at the start of each meeting for open dialogue – no agenda, just questions. Over time, this ritual creates a space where staff feel safe to raise challenges, share uncertainties, and test new ideas. When a new assessment framework is introduced, the conversation doesn't begin with 'How do we implement this?' but with 'What are we learning about our students through this?' That shift – from implementation to inquiry – isn't accidental. It's a product of leadership that listens.

Leadership also means knowing when to get out of the way. In some of the most adaptive schools I've worked with, principals spoke the least in staff meetings. Their role was not to provide answers, but to host the dialogue – to ensure the voices of teachers were heard, and that conversations stayed anchored in student learning. As Harris and Jones (2015) emphasise, in high-performing schools, leadership is 'nested' within professional learning communities, where collective efficacy becomes the engine of improvement.

Leadership that listens is also leadership that learns. It remains open to challenge. It welcomes disagreement as a sign of engagement, not defiance. It resists the urge to tidy things up too quickly. Fullan and Quinn (2016) argue that coherence in education is not about linearity, but about shared understanding. And shared understanding is built through dialogue, not directives.

In practical terms, this kind of leadership requires courage. It takes courage to hold the line on collaboration when the system demands quick wins; to slow down and reflect when policy incentives push for speed; to protect teachers' time for learning when the timetable is already crowded. But it is precisely these choices that shape a culture in which curiosity can survive.

Perhaps the most vital role of the leader in a curious school is to hold the tension between *urgency* and *inquiry* – to remind the community that we can move quickly, but only in service of learning, not in place of it; that results matter, but not at the cost of relationships; that curiosity is not a distraction from improvement – it is the engine of it.

When leaders listen, others begin to speak. When they reflect, others feel safe to question. And when they model learning, they give permission for the whole school to do the same.

Systems that support, not suppress

If culture and leadership form the inner scaffolding of a curious school, then the wider system in which that school operates must also be designed to sustain – not stifle – curiosity. This is often where the greatest tension lies. For even the most inspired schools can be flattened by systems that reward speed, certainty, and conformity over reflection, nuance, and learning.

Curiosity struggles in systems that overreach. Where everything is measured and audited, there is little room for experimentation. Educators become cautious, performative, and risk-averse. Feedback becomes surveillance. Reflection is narrowed to what can be counted. But the problem isn't only overreach – it's also detachment. When systems step back too far, they leave schools isolated and unsupported. Improvement becomes dependent on local leadership capacity or luck. Excellence becomes an accident, not a pattern.

Embedding curiosity at scale, then, depends on a different kind of system – one that sees itself as a learning ecosystem. Systems that support curiosity do not impose change or abandon responsibility. Instead, they design for learning at scale. They ask: *How do we make it easier for schools to inquire, reflect, and adapt? What conditions are necessary for schools to improve themselves – together?*

Peter Senge (1990) described learning organisations as those 'where people continually expand their capacity to create the results they truly desire'. Systems that support school improvement must operate in the same spirit. They must prioritise learning at every level – student, teacher, school, and system – and align their practices to reinforce it.

There are signs of this in systems that strike the right balance between accountability and autonomy. Ontario's school system, for instance, became globally recognised not through rigid mandates but through collaborative capacity-building and focused, trust-based leadership (Sharratt & Fullan, 2009). Finland's education success is underpinned by deep trust in teacher professionalism, coupled with a system that supports equitable outcomes across diverse communities (Sahlberg, 2016). These systems have done more than pass good policy; they have invested in building school capital across all levels – ensuring that trust, time, expertise, and collaborative capacity are in place to support sustained inquiry. Even Singapore, known for its high performance, has shifted in recent years toward innovation, flexibility, and teacher-led design.

These systems share several characteristics:
- **They fund time for deep professional learning.** They recognise that collaboration and inquiry are not luxuries, but necessities for sustained improvement.
- **They build feedback loops.** Through peer networks, learning communities, and shared data reflection, they enable educators to learn from one another – not just from the centre.
- **They avoid 'initiative overload'.** Instead of constantly introducing new programs, they focus on building adaptive capacity within schools.
- **They protect professional trust.** Rather than defaulting to compliance, they use trust as a lever for responsibility and growth.

In the Australian context, the challenge is stark. Despite pockets of innovation and leadership excellence, national policy has too often prioritised measurement over meaning. As Jensen (2013) and Gonski et al. (2018) have argued, Australia's education reform agenda has struggled to translate funding and rhetoric into sustained, system-wide equity or innovation. The result is a persistent gap between what schools are expected to do and what they are enabled to do.

To move forward, systems must shift from driving change to scaffolding curiosity. That means creating space in policies for inquiry. It means resourcing coaching and collaboration – not just content delivery. It means resisting the impulse to mandate and instead investing in trust-rich partnerships between schools and government.

And it means recognising that curiosity is not fragile – it is foundational. When teachers are trusted to learn together, they get better. When schools are supported to think deeply, they find answers. When systems stop rushing and start listening, they discover that reflection isn't slow – it's efficient. It saves time downstream. It prevents reactive cycles. It builds depth.

Curious systems do not see schools as delivery units. They see them as learning communities. And they know that if the system learns – if it really learns – it doesn't need to control every move. It just needs to set the conditions for growth.

But sustaining curiosity is not only about how systems are designed – it is also about how inquiry is lived each day, through the patterns of practice that shape the life of a school.

Practices that pattern inquiry

If culture is the heartbeat of a curious school, and leadership the rhythm, then practices are the pulse – the daily actions through which curiosity is lived, not just spoken. These practices don't need to be complex. In fact, the most powerful ones are often deceptively simple. What matters is that they are consistent, intentional, and patterned into the everyday life of the school.

In curious schools, inquiry is not episodic. It doesn't appear only on planning days or during pilot projects. It is threaded through the week, woven into conversations, and reflected in the routines that guide both teacher and student learning. Over time, these repeated practices become cultural habits – not formulas, but rhythms; predictable enough to be trusted, and flexible enough to evolve.

This is what distinguishes surface curiosity from sustained inquiry. As Timperley et al. (2007) found in their analysis of professional learning, it is not one-off initiatives that lead to meaningful improvement, but those that engage teachers in sustained cycles of learning, reflection, and adaptation. In other words, *practice becomes improvement* when it is inquiry-driven and repeated with purpose.

Consider some examples:

- **Inquiry cycles** – short, focused cycles of planning, action, observation, and reflection – help teams test changes in teaching practice. The simplicity of these cycles is their strength. They offer a structure for curiosity to flourish, especially when framed around student learning. Teachers ask: 'What are we trying? What are we seeing? What will we do next?'
- **Structured peer observation**, when designed around questions rather than judgments, enables teachers to learn from each other in real classrooms. When peers observe not to evaluate, but to notice patterns and reflect together, professional growth becomes a collective act. Feedback becomes a shared responsibility.
- **Learning story exchanges** – brief, structured times where staff share stories of student growth, challenge, or surprise – building a sense of shared purpose and insight. These stories reconnect teachers to the moral core of their work. They make curiosity visible and purposeful.
- **Protocols for making student thinking visible**, such as thinking routines (Ritchhart et al., 2011), anchor curiosity in the learner's world.

They help teachers shift from asking 'Did they get it?' to 'How are they thinking?' This fosters deeper pedagogical inquiry and surfaces rich, formative data.

These practices, once embedded, reshape how teachers think about their work. They shift the default setting from *delivery* to *discovery*. They encourage pattern recognition – noticing what works, when, and for whom. This aligns with research in cognitive science, which shows that pattern recognition is a hallmark of expert thinking (Bransford et al., 2000). In schools, these patterns are not memorised – they are co-constructed through collaborative, curious practice.

Importantly, the practices themselves are not the point. The *pattern* is. What matters is that these routines make inquiry predictable. They send a signal: *In this school, we ask questions. We reflect. We learn together.*

This predictability supports psychological safety. As Edmondson (2019) has shown, teams perform best when people feel safe to share uncertainty and risk failure. Consistent inquiry practices normalise that vulnerability. They make it easier for teachers to say, 'I'm not sure this worked' or 'What did you notice in your class?'

Over time, this patterning makes the school more adaptive. When external conditions shift – policy changes, new leadership, funding fluctuations – curious schools are less destabilised. Their improvement isn't dependent on external programs; it is driven by internal rhythms. This is what Mitchell and Sackney (2011) called *the capacity for self-renewal* – the ability of schools to keep learning, even as the landscape changes.

It is tempting to chase novelty in school improvement. But innovation without rhythm is noise. The schools that sustain curiosity are not always the flashiest. But they are the ones that keep learning – not sporadically, but consistently. Day after day. Question after question. Pattern after pattern.

Anchored in purpose

Curiosity is powerful. But without purpose, it can drift.

In schools, curiosity without a moral anchor can become indulgent – fascinated by novelty, distracted by ideas, content to tinker rather than transform. The most enduring inquiry, however, is not aimless. It is directed. It is disciplined by a deeper reason to learn. In the schools described throughout this book, curiosity does not float freely. It is tethered to something larger: a shared commitment to making education better *for all students.*

When curiosity is anchored in moral purpose, it becomes more than an intellectual exercise. It becomes a force for equity, for justice, for human dignity. Educators are no longer asking 'What's interesting?' They are asking 'What's right?' They want to understand why some students are thriving and others are not. They seek to uncover how classroom practice, school structures, or systemic forces might be unintentionally reproducing inequality – and how those patterns might be disrupted. They are learning, not just for the sake of learning, but because they care deeply about the lives they touch.

This fusion of excellence and ethics is central to what Gardner et al. (2001) call 'Good Work' – work that is excellent in quality, personally meaningful, and socially responsible. In education, good work means teaching not only effectively but ethically. It means using curiosity to challenge assumptions, examine consequences, and rethink habits that no longer serve our students. Without this moral compass, curiosity risks becoming superficial. With it, inquiry becomes revolutionary.

Schools that ground curiosity in moral purpose consistently ask hard questions: Whose voices are missing in our curriculum? Which students are being disciplined more harshly, or included less often? Where are our biases showing up in assessment or engagement? These are not easy conversations. But they are essential if inquiry is to serve the whole child – and the whole community.

Fullan and Quinn (2016) argue that coherence emerges when purpose, practice, and pedagogy align. In curious schools, this alignment is explicit. Purpose drives the questions that are asked. It shapes the data that is collected, the stories that are told, the priorities that are chosen. Curiosity becomes less about individual innovation and more about collective transformation.

This is especially important in contexts of disadvantage. In low-SES schools, curiosity can be a disruptive force – challenging deficit narratives, resisting fatalism, and pushing back against the structural inertia that often frames disadvantage as destiny. When leaders and teachers in these schools embrace inquiry with moral purpose, they do so not to survive, but to reimagine. They ask, again and again: 'What is possible here? For these students? In this community?'

Anchored in purpose, curiosity becomes not just a habit of mind but a stance of hope. It signals belief – that change is possible, that all students are capable, and that schools can be places of deep human flourishing.

What endures

Curiosity brought us here. But as this final chapter draws to a close, the question is no longer just 'What sparks curiosity?' – it is 'How can curiosity remain a living force in the school?' What survives once the applause fades, once the initiative ends, once the energy dips and the urgency of day-to-day school life takes over again?

This book has argued that what endures is not a single program, framework, or leader. It is a way of working – curious, collaborative, purposeful. It is a belief that schools are not static institutions delivering fixed content, but dynamic learning communities capable of growth, reflection, and transformation. It is the commitment to come together, again and again, to ask: 'What are we learning? What are we seeing? What might we do differently next time?'

That commitment – anchored in moral purpose, supported by strong leadership, and underpinned by rich school capital – is what lasts. Not because it is always easy or glamorous, but because it is resilient. Because it can bend without breaking. Because it grows stronger over time.

The most enduring schools are not immune to pressure or politics. They are not untouched by funding cuts, policy churn, or staff turnover. But they are sustained by something deeper. A rhythm. A story. A shared sense of *why*. They remember that improvement is not only about delivery – it is about *becoming*. Becoming more attuned to learners. More responsive to change. More alive to possibility.

bell hooks (1994) reminds us that education can be the practice of freedom. And freedom, in this context, does not mean unbounded autonomy or the absence of structure. It means the freedom to inquire, to imagine, and to act in ways that serve students with depth and care. Schools that embody this practice are not always dramatic in their innovation. But they are steady in their intention.

In these schools, curiosity becomes a generative force. It ripples outward – from teachers to teams, from classrooms to leadership, from the local to the system. And while the tools may change – new protocols, new research, new approaches – the underlying spirit does not. It is a spirit of collective responsibility, of patient attention, of hopeful disruption.

This is where the Curious Cat, our quiet companion throughout this journey, finds its place again. Not as a gimmick or a mascot, but as a symbol. A reminder that transformation often begins not with a declaration, but with a question. That improvement is not a sprint, but a pattern of return. That the real engine of change is not novelty, but meaning.

The Cat does not need to be centre stage. It lingers, watches, listens. It nudges gently when the routine becomes rote, when the script becomes stale, when the answers feel too polished. It asks, 'What else?' and 'Why not?' and sometimes, 'What if we're wrong?' In doing so, it keeps the work alive.

In one school, a student asked the teacher, 'Why do we always start with a question instead of an answer?' The teacher smiled and said, 'Because the question is where learning begins.' That moment – a glance, a spark, a shift – is what endures. Not the slogan. Not the structure. But the act of inquiry, repeated, renewed, and shared.

The Curious Cat leaves us here – not with closure, but with continuation. Not at the end of a journey, but at a new threshold. Because curiosity, once awakened, does not sleep for long. It returns – in staffrooms, in classrooms, in the voice of a child asking 'Why?'

And so, the work goes on. Quiet. Vital. Very much alive.

A thought-provoker for lasting practice

'In the end, what remains is not the program, but the pattern. Not the tool, but the trust.'

In a culture saturated with initiatives, frameworks, and performance cycles, endurance is not about clinging to structures – it's about growing a way of being. This provoker invites individuals or teams to reflect on the deeper patterns that sustain school improvement beyond the headlines, the hype, and the hurry.

Consider this ...

1. What do we return to when the strategy fades, the funding ends, or the leader moves on?
2. Where does our school show signs of 'rhythmic integrity' – actions we take not because we're told to but because they reflect who we are?

3. What stories in our school community are worth retelling – not because they're polished, but because they reveal something enduring about our purpose?
4. When the urgent overshadows the important, what helps us return to what matters most?
5. If we disappeared tomorrow, what would others say lived here – beyond our results, programs, or reputation?

A reflective frame

Use the following sentence stems to prompt written reflection or dialogue:

- 'In our school, what holds us steady is …'
- 'We know we're on track when we notice …'
- 'Even when things get hard, we still …'
- 'The most enduring part of our culture is …'

> **Closing thought**
>
> *'The strongest schools are not those that never falter –
> but those that remember why they began.'*
>
> Let this be your compass – not just what works, but what lasts.

From insight to action: sustaining a movement over time

Sustaining curiosity-led improvement is not about chasing novelty – it is about embedding a culture of questioning, reflection, and ethical action that endures through change. This work is never finished. But it can be renewed, and it can grow.

For teachers:

- Keep a personal inquiry journal – what questions are emerging in your practice?
- Create reflective routines with colleagues – what are we noticing about learning this term? What next?
- Model curiosity openly with students – curiosity is caught, not just taught.

For principals:

- Celebrate stories of curiosity and moral purpose in your school – make these visible and valued.
- Build succession with curiosity in mind – how are we growing the next generation of inquiry-driven leaders?
- Protect time and space for reflection, even in busy cycles – the urgent must not always crowd out the important.

For systems:

- Encourage 'slow work' – create room for deep, long-term inquiry alongside short-term targets.
- Invest in leadership development that cultivates inquiry, adaptive expertise, and moral clarity – not just technical compliance.
- Keep asking: What rhythms, rituals, and relationships will help this work outlast this year, this plan, this leadership term?

Curiosity that endures is not about chasing the next big thing – it is about asking better questions, together, again and again. That is how the system grows. That is how the Cat keeps walking.

The Cat lingers at the edge of the staffroom. Not waiting for applause, just watching. A question forms. A teacher leans forward. A student asks, 'Why?' And in that moment, the work continues – quiet, vital, and very much alive.

Afterword: introducing new thinking

This chapter has challenged the idea that scaling requires replication. It has shown that systems grow not by imposing blueprints but by cultivating cultures – of trust, reflection, and shared purpose. Scaling inquiry is not about creating carbon copies of high-performing schools. It is about enabling each school to become a place of thoughtful learning, in its own context and community.

To do this, systems must attend as much to the *how* as to the *what*. Structures matter, but only if they are animated by curiosity and sustained by care. Policy matters, but only when it invites rather than dictates. Networks matter, but only when they are anchored in shared moral purpose and grounded in the realities of everyday practice. They also rely on school capital – the conditions that allow inquiry to be enacted meaningfully, not just imagined. Without strong professional relationships, time for reflection, and organisational trust, curiosity withers.

The central argument is simple but vital: curiosity can scale – not as a program, but as a way of working. When the right conditions are in place, inquiry spreads. When systems honour the intelligence of the field, trust deepens. And when learning is protected at every level, improvement becomes something we grow into – not something we chase.

Scaling with integrity means asking, again and again: Are we learning, or are we delivering? Are we building coherence, or just compliance? Are we stewarding curiosity – or stifling it?

These are questions not just for systems, but for the people who shape them: for teachers, leaders, and policy-makers alike.

And so, the Curious Cat takes one last glance – not back, but forward. Watching for signs that the culture is shifting, that dialogue is deepening, that inquiry is travelling. Not because someone mandated it, but because people believe in it.

The next chapter of this story is not written here. It will be written in your practice, your leadership, your system. Quietly. Collectively. And with curiosity at the core.

And the Cat's next step? Now, it seems, that is ours to take.

EPILOGUE
In the Company of Questions

'Hope is not the conviction that something will turn out well, but the certainty that something is worth doing, no matter how it turns out.'
– Václav Havel

Improvement doesn't begin with certainty. It begins with curiosity – with someone asking, 'What if?', 'Why not?', or 'What are we missing?'

Throughout this book, we've explored how schools can reclaim curiosity, not just as an individual trait but as a collective habit – a way of leading, teaching, learning, and organising.

We've seen that curiosity alone isn't enough. It needs conditions – the capital of the school – to take root. It needs moral purpose to stay focused on equity and justice. And it needs leadership that protects and provokes, especially in systems built for compliance.

This view is supported by growing research: that teacher agency and collective efficacy (Hargreaves & Fullan, 2012), relational trust (Bryk & Schneider, 2002), and professional inquiry (Timperley et al., 2007) are among the most powerful levers for school improvement. The findings in this book add to that literature, showing that curiosity – in both teachers and systems – is not a distraction from performance, but a pathway to it.

But change isn't driven by citations. It's driven by conviction. And by practice. And by people asking better questions of themselves, their students, their colleagues, and their communities.

This isn't a book of answers. It's a book of invitations – to pause, to rethink, to reconnect.

And the Curious Cat? It doesn't exit with a bow. It lingers – on the edge of the meeting, in the margin of a unit plan, in the silence before someone says: 'I'm not sure – but let's find out.'

Because the work isn't finished – and the best questions are still to come.

APPENDIX A
Research Summary and Methodology

This book is based on the author's doctoral thesis, *The Curious Cat and the Quest for School Improvement: Unpacking the Impact on Student Learning of School SES, Workplace Curiosity, Moral Purpose, and School Capital*, University of Melbourne (Craig, 2025).

This explored how school improvement is influenced by three powerful forces: **workplace curiosity**, **moral purpose**, and **school capital** - all in the shadow of one of education's most persistent challenges: **school socioeconomic status (SES)**.

1. The research problem

For decades, studies have shown that school SES is the most consistent predictor of student achievement. Yet policy efforts to reduce this effect have often produced only incremental gains. At the same time, qualities like curiosity, moral purpose, and professional capital - while widely discussed - have been underexplored as potential levers for deep, equitable, and scalable school improvement.

The central question that guided this research was: To what extent do workplace curiosity, moral purpose, and school capital influence student learning outcomes in Australian schools - especially when controlling for SES?

2. Conceptual framework

The study drew on three interrelated theoretical pillars:

- **Workplace curiosity** – Drawing from Todd Kashdan's multidimensional model, curiosity was treated not just as a student trait but as an adult

disposition: the professional stance educators take toward change, learning, and complexity.
- **Moral purpose** – Inspired by the work of Michael Fullan, Michael Barber, David Hopkins and the Good Work Project (Gardner et al., 2001), moral purpose was framed as the educator's ethical drive to make a meaningful difference in students' lives.
- **School capital** – Based on frameworks developed by Hargreaves (2001), and later expanded by Caldwell and Harris (2008), school capital was treated as a multidimensional construct, encompassing intellectual, social, organisational, and financial capital.

Together, these forces were analysed not only for their individual impact but for how they interact and operate under different SES conditions.

3. Data collection and participants

The study involved **829 educators** across **42 schools** in four Australian states: **South Australia**, **Tasmania**, **Queensland**, and **Victoria**. Participants included school leaders, classroom teachers, and specialist staff from both primary and secondary settings.

Schools were selected to represent a wide range of SES profiles, enabling an exploration of how the constructs functioned in both advantaged and disadvantaged contexts.

Data were collected through a **comprehensive survey instrument** comprising validated scales and newly developed items. These included:
- The **Workplace Curiosity Scale** (Kashdan et al., 2020)
- Moral Purpose from the Spiritual Capital indicators from the framework by Caldwell and Harris (2008)
- A 22-item School Capital instrument from the framework by Caldwell and Harris (2008)
- Five-year student learning outcomes and school SES level as reported by the MySchool website.

4. Analytical methods

The research employed both **standard linear regression** and **hierarchical regression modelling**. This approach enabled the analysis of both individual-level relationships (for example, how a teacher's curiosity might relate to learning outcomes) and school-level dynamics (for example, how capital interacts with SES to influence performance).

The modelling addressed three key questions:

1. How much of the variance in student learning can be explained by workplace curiosity, moral purpose, and school capital – individually and together?
2. How do these variables interact with **school SES**?
3. Which combination of factors provides the strongest predictive power for **equitable, sustainable improvement**?

5. Key findings

The results were both confirming and surprising:

- SES remained the strongest single predictor of student outcomes, but it was not deterministic.
- Workplace curiosity alone had limited direct impact on student learning, but its effect was significantly amplified when coupled with high levels of moral purpose and capital.
- Moral purpose showed a strong positive relationship with perceived student outcomes, especially in schools with lower SES.
- School capital emerged as the most significant modifiable factor – particularly intellectual and organisational capital, which enabled inquiry, collaboration, and adaptive leadership.
- The most powerful improvement occurred when all three factors were **aligned** and **reinforced across the school**.

These findings suggest that curiosity must be seen not as an individual trait or a pedagogical strategy, but as a **collective disposition** – one that thrives only when purpose is shared and capital is strong.

6. Implications for practice

The research affirmed what many educators know instinctively: real improvement is not achieved through quick fixes or performance mandates. It comes when curiosity is protected, when purpose is shared, and when schools have the capital to act on both. For policy-makers, the study offers a call to design systems that **support learning, not just measure it**. For school leaders, it offers a pathway to culture, not just strategy. And for teachers, it reclaims curiosity as a **professional right and responsibility** – not a luxury.

7. Connection to the book

This book is both inspired by and extends beyond the research. While the empirical study provided the evidence base, the book blends those insights with **narrative, metaphor, and lived leadership experience** – translating complex findings into actionable, real-world change. The Curious Cat is more than a character. It is a call to rethink improvement, not as compliance but as a dance of purpose, capital, and curiosity – within every school, and across the whole system.

APPENDIX B

Implementation Guides

Guide for curious practice: for students

Wonder more. Think deeper. Ask better.

Curiosity is more than asking questions – it's about how you see the world and how you choose to learn. Every student can be curious. And every question can lead to something new.

Here's how you can build your curious practice:

1. Stay open to wonder

- Look for the unusual, the unexplained, the surprising.
- Ask yourself: 'What's something here I haven't noticed before?'
- Use 'What if …?' and 'Why does …?' to start your thinking.

Try this: Make a daily *wonder list* – at school, at home, on the bus.

2. Ask brave questions

- Don't wait for permission to be curious.
- There are no 'silly' questions – only starting points for learning.
- Dig deeper: move from 'What is it?' to 'How does it work?' and 'Why does it matter?'

Try this: After each lesson, ask yourself: 'What do I still want to know?'

3. Make learning yours

- Connect what you're learning to things you care about.
- Explore beyond the textbook – podcasts, museums, family stories, the natural world.
- Choose projects or inquiry questions that matter to *you*.

Try this: Keep a curiosity journal or digital folder of ideas you want to explore.

4. Look sideways

- Be curious about others – not just ideas.
- Ask classmates: 'How did you solve that? What did you think about this?'
- Learn from different opinions, cultures, and experiences.

Try this: In group work, take turns asking each other curiosity questions – not just answers.

5. Be okay with not knowing (yet)

- Learning takes time.
- It's okay to feel confused or stuck – it means your brain is working.
- Practise saying: 'I don't know ... but I want to find out.'

Try this: Write down three things you didn't know last week ... and how you learned them.

6. Build habits that last

- Start and end your day with a question.
- When you read, don't just underline – *interrogate*.
- Use sticky notes, visual maps, or question walls to track your wondering.

Try this: Challenge yourself to ask five thoughtful questions in each subject this term.

7. Stay curious about people

- Everyone has a story. Ask questions with kindness and respect.
- Be interested in what makes others think, feel, and dream.
- Listen to learn – not just to reply.

Try this: Interview a family member or teacher about what made them curious as a child.

Remember: Curiosity isn't just for school. It's how you shape the kind of person you want to become. Keep wondering. Keep questioning. Keep growing.

Guide for curious practice: for parents and carers

Nurturing curiosity, one question at a time

Curious children grow into thoughtful, creative adults. But curiosity doesn't just happen at school – it begins and grows at home. As a parent, you play a powerful role in shaping how your child sees the world.

This guide offers practical ways to support curiosity in everyday family life.

1. Ask open-ended questions

Instead of 'Did you have a good day?', try:

- 'What made you think today?'
- 'Did anything surprise you?'
- 'What question did you ask at school?'

Tip: Focus less on finding the 'right' answer and more on exploring the idea together.

2. Model curiosity

Show your own interest in learning, even if it's small.

- Say, 'I've always wondered …' or 'I read something interesting today.'
- Share questions you don't know the answer to – and find out together.

Tip: Let your child see you researching, reflecting, or puzzling over things.

3. Follow their fascinations

Notice what lights your child up – whether it's dinosaurs, baking, outer space, or bugs. Then:

- Help them explore deeper: books, YouTube clips, museums, backyard experiments.
- Encourage projects that stem from their questions.

Tip: Curiosity doesn't have to be 'academic' to be meaningful.

4. Celebrate the questions, not just the results

If your child asks a great question, praise their thinking – whether or not it leads to an answer.

- Say, 'That's a thoughtful question,' or 'I love how your brain works.'
- Make it normal to say 'I don't know – let's find out.'

Tip: Ask 'What do you think?' before giving an answer.

5. Build curiosity into family life
- Keep a family 'Wonder Wall' or notebook for big questions.
- Have one screen-free meal a week with a conversation starter like:
  - 'If animals could talk, what would you ask them?'
  - 'What invention would make your life easier?'

Tip: Use car rides, mealtimes, or bedtime for open conversations.

6. Encourage (safe) risk-taking and creativity
- Let kids try things out – even if messy or imperfect.
- Avoid jumping in with solutions. Let them struggle productively.
- Encourage experimentation: new recipes, recycled art, made-up games.

Tip: Curiosity grows when kids feel safe to try and fail.

7. Stay curious about your child
- Ask what they care about – and really listen.
- Be curious about how they see the world.
- Avoid assuming you already know what they think or feel.

Tip: Ask 'What do you wish teachers knew about how you learn?'

Curiosity starts with connection

When children feel seen, heard, and safe, their natural curiosity flourishes. You don't need all the answers. You just need to share the journey.

Keep asking. Keep listening. Keep learning – together.

Guide for curious practice: for teachers

Teaching as inquiry, learning as wonder

Curiosity isn't an add-on – it's the energy behind powerful teaching and learning. When teachers model and protect curiosity, they transform classrooms into spaces of exploration, reflection, and growth.

This guide supports teachers in reawakening curiosity – for themselves and their students.

1. Start with a question, not a script

- Design learning experiences around open-ended provocations: 'What might happen if …?' or 'Why do you think …?'
- Use inquiry cycles: notice → wonder → try → reflect → adapt.

AI, like ChatGPT, can be a valuable starting point if you're short on ideas.

Tip: A rich question can carry a week of learning more than a packed unit plan.

2. Teach with students, not just to them

- Co-construct learning goals and rubrics.
- Invite students to frame their own questions and choose inquiry paths.
- Use formative feedback as a shared reflection, not a judgment.

Tip: Ask students, 'What's puzzling you right now?' and build from there.

3. Protect your own professional curiosity

- Take time to explore new ideas, research, or practices.
- Set one 'practice puzzle' each term: 'What am I trying to improve, and why?'
- Keep a simple learning journal or wonder wall.

Tip: Use the phrase 'I'm experimenting with …' in team meetings to normalise inquiry.

4. Talk about practice, not just planning

- Use planning time to ask: 'What are we noticing about our students?'
- Share what didn't work – not just successes.
- In walkthroughs, focus on questions: 'What might we tweak next time?'

Tip: Reframe 'evaluation' as 'evidence for learning – ours and theirs.'

5. Design for thinking
- Offer learning tasks that provoke curiosity:
    - Conceptual provocations
    - Real-world dilemmas
    - Design challenges
- Allow space for ambiguity and reflection – not just pace and coverage.

Tip: Students learn deeply when they don't know exactly what comes next.

6. Build a culture of safe risk-taking
- Model your own learning stumbles: 'Here's what I tried – and what I learned.'
- Encourage students to reframe mistakes as part of thinking, not failure.
- Use routines like 'I used to think … now I think …' to show growth.

Tip: Curiosity needs safety. Safety grows through relationships.

7. Stay professionally alive
- Observe a colleague teach – then debrief as learners, not judges.
- Join a professional network or inquiry group, even informally.

Tip: Professional curiosity is contagious – start where the energy is.

Teaching is a thinking profession

Curious teachers ask:

- What's really going on with this student?
- Why did that strategy land – or fall flat?
- What do I need to unlearn?
- How might I do this differently next time?

You don't need perfect answers. You need the courage to keep asking the right questions.

Guide for curious practice: for principals

Leadership as inquiry, culture as curiosity

Leadership that centres curiosity doesn't impose direction – it opens space. Curious principals lead with questions, build trust through inquiry, and model the kind of learning they want to see in their schools.

This guide supports principals to embed curiosity into leadership practice, staff culture, and school-wide learning.

1. Lead with questions, not just goals

- Ask: 'What are we learning?' – not just 'What are we doing?'
- Start improvement conversations with wonder: 'What are we noticing?' 'Where is energy building?' 'What's emerging that deserves our attention?'

Tip: Strategic plans grounded in curiosity remain adaptive and alive.

2. Listen with intention

- Protect time to listen deeply to students, staff, families, and your leadership team.
- Ask teachers, 'What puzzles are you working on in your practice?'
- Treat staff voice as formative data – not feedback for performance management, but insight for shared reflection.

Tip: The best principals listen more than they speak – and reflect more than they react.

3. Make reflection a leadership habit

- Use weekly journals or leadership huddles to reflect on: 'What surprised me this week?' 'What might I be missing?' 'Where is curiosity being modelled – and where is it missing?'
- Ask 'what did we learn?' in every review, not just 'how did we perform?'

Tip: Leading is learning. Protect time for your own inquiry, not just others'.

4. Design staff culture that thinks together
- Create staff meeting routines that begin with questions or provocations.
- Embed inquiry cycles into team planning and appraisal conversations.
- Promote low-risk experimentation: 'Try, reflect, share.'

Tip: Inquiry cultures grow when thinking is made visible – and non-judgmental.

5. Position professional learning as exploration
- Shift PD from 'delivery' to co-construction: 'What do we want to understand more deeply?' 'What's the best question we could be asking together right now?'
- Invite staff to lead learning from their practice.

Tip: When teachers bring puzzles, not just problems, growth multiplies.

6. Use data as a conversation starter, not a scorecard
- Ask: 'What's the story behind this pattern?' 'What's missing from this data?' 'How do our students experience this trend?'
- Use multiple forms of evidence: voice, narrative, observation, and outcomes.

Tip: Curious data practices are relational, not reductive.

7. Protect the conditions for curiosity
- Defend thinking time in meeting agendas.
- Use walkthroughs to notice patterns, not evaluate individuals.
- Give teams permission to say 'We don't know yet – but we're finding out.'

Tip: Curiosity thrives where safety, time, and purpose intersect.

Curious leadership is relational, responsive, reflective

Principals who lead with curiosity ...

- Invite staff to explore, not just implement.
- Build coherence through shared inquiry, not compliance.
- Help the school ask: 'What matters most now?' and 'How might we grow into it?'

Curiosity isn't a soft skill – it's the strategy behind sustainable improvement.

Guide for curious practice: for system leaders

Scaling trust, learning, and inquiry

Curious systems are built by leaders who treat learning as their central work – not just for students, but for schools and systems themselves. These leaders don't just drive reform. They ask better questions, build conditions for professional trust, and design architecture that listens.

This guide supports system leaders to centre curiosity as a driver of equity, improvement, and culture.

1. Start with questions, not solutions

- Ask: 'What do we not yet understand about our schools?' 'What are our schools noticing that we aren't?' 'Where is energy building – and what can we learn from it?'

Tip: Great systems don't start with blueprints. They start with listening.

2. Make system intelligence collective

- Build inquiry teams or learning networks across schools, roles, and regions.
- Create mechanisms where frontline educators shape strategy (for example, learning reviews, field design labs).
- Use collective insight – not just policy teams – to adapt priorities.

Tip: Smart systems aren't more technical – they're more relational.

3. Use data to generate insight, not control

- Diversify your definition of evidence: include narrative, voice, local case studies, and field observations.
- Replace inspection-style reviews with collaborative learning walks and networked reflection.
- Ask: 'What's the story behind this data?' and 'What questions should we be asking now?'

Tip: When systems ask better questions, schools trust them more.

4. Build learning partnerships, not pipelines

- Shift relationships from delivery chains to co-learning ecosystems.
- Co-create professional learning with principals, teachers, and communities.

- Invest in partnerships with researchers, cultural institutions, and families – not just vendors.

Tip: Insight scales when trust and connection do.

5. Align policy with purpose and inquiry

- Design policy that guides without dictating.
- Build frameworks that ask: 'What kind of learning are we enabling?' 'How does this policy protect time for thinking?' 'Are we inviting experimentation – or just enforcement?'

Tip: Curious policy names the 'why' and trusts schools with the 'how'.

6. Model curiosity in system leadership

- Treat executive meetings as learning spaces, not performance tables.
- Begin each strategy cycle with an inquiry: 'What are we learning from the field?'
- Host forums where leaders reflect aloud on mistakes, insights, and uncertainty.

Tip: System leaders set the tone – curiosity starts at the top.

7. Protect the conditions for school-level inquiry

- Fund collaborative time, not just programs.
- Reduce initiative overload – create 'slack' for schools to explore, adapt, and reflect.
- Ensure accountability reviews include school-led stories, not just top-down metrics.

Tip: System pressure without system trust chokes innovation.

Curious systems learn – they don't just deliver

System leaders who practise curiosity ...

- Build trust by listening more than they mandate.
- Scale inquiry by investing in networks and shared reflection.
- Design architecture that adapts – not just implements.

Curiosity at scale isn't a luxury. It's how systems stay intelligent, just, and alive to possibility.

Curious systems grow not through mandates, but through trust and learning. As a system leader, your questions, your listening, and your choices help shape the culture where curiosity can thrive.

APPENDIX C
Self-Reflection Tools

Self-reflection tool for curious students

Questions are where learning begins.

This reflection tool helps you think about how you learn – not just what you know. Curiosity isn't about having all the answers. It's about wanting to find out more, to explore, to ask *why* and *what if…?*

Use the prompts below to reflect on your learning habits, interests, and mindset.

My approach to learning

How do I usually feel when I'm learning something new?

- ☐ Excited
- ☐ Nervous
- ☐ Bored
- ☐ Curious
- ☐ Confused
- ☐ A mix of these

When something gets hard, I tend to …

- ☐ Keep trying
- ☐ Ask for help
- ☐ Avoid it
- ☐ Break it into smaller steps
- ☐ Get frustrated

One thing I'm proud of in my learning this term is:

_____

My curiosity in action

I ask questions when …

- ☐ I'm interested in the topic
- ☐ I don't understand
- ☐ I want to go deeper
- ☐ I notice something unusual
- ☐ I feel confident
- ☐ I feel safe to speak up

An interesting question I've asked recently is:

_____

A topic or idea I'd love to learn more about is:

_____

My learning relationships

I learn best when …

- ☐ I work alone
- ☐ I talk with others
- ☐ I have examples
- ☐ I can move around
- ☐ I teach someone else
- ☐ I make something

Who helps me be curious in my learning?

- ☐ My teacher
- ☐ A friend or classmate
- ☐ My family
- ☐ A mentor
- ☐ Myself

Someone I've learned from recently is …

_____

Thinking about thinking

When I make a mistake, I usually …

- ☐ Feel embarrassed
- ☐ Try to fix it
- ☐ Ask why it happened
- ☐ Give up
- ☐ Learn from it

One way I can stretch my thinking is to …

_____

I feel most curious when I'm …

- ☐ Creating something
- ☐ Solving a real problem
- ☐ Exploring my own ideas
- ☐ Connecting learning to my life
- ☐ Outside of school
- ☐ Working with others

Setting a curious goal

One question I want to explore this term is:

_____

One thing I can try to stay curious this week is:

_____

Someone I'd like to share my learning with is:

_____

Remember: Being curious isn't about being right – it's about being open. Keep asking, keep wondering, keep learning.

Self-reflection tool for curious parenting

Curiosity grows best when families wonder together.

This tool invites you to reflect on how your own habits, questions, and interactions support your child's curiosity and love of learning.

Curiosity doesn't require expert answers. It thrives on everyday moments of wonder, listening, and shared exploration.

How my child approaches learning

When my child is learning something new, they usually …

- ☐ Ask a lot of questions
- ☐ Want to try it straight away
- ☐ Get easily frustrated
- ☐ Stay focused
- ☐ Lose interest quickly
- ☐ Need encouragement

One thing I've noticed about how they learn best is:

_____

One thing they've been really curious about lately is:

_____

Our family learning habits

In our home, learning happens through …

- ☐ Conversations around the dinner table
- ☐ Storytelling or reading together
- ☐ Problem-solving in daily tasks
- ☐ Exploring nature or the world outside
- ☐ Games, projects, or creative time
- ☐ Technology and online tools

We make time to talk about school and learning:

- ☐ Daily
- ☐ A few times a week
- ☐ When something goes wrong
- ☐ Not as often as I'd like

One small routine that helps curiosity at home is:

_____

How I respond to questions

When my child asks a tricky or unexpected question, I usually …

- ☐ Try to give a clear answer
- ☐ Say 'let's look that up'
- ☐ Encourage them to think it through
- ☐ Change the subject
- ☐ Feel unsure how to respond

One recent question my child asked that made me think was:

___

How did I respond? What might I do next time?

___

Encouraging curiosity

I support my child's curiosity by …

- ☐ Asking questions back
- ☐ Listening without rushing
- ☐ Valuing mistakes as part of learning
- ☐ Helping them find answers
- ☐ Letting them lead the way sometimes
- ☐ Noticing what they love

Something I could do more often to support curiosity is:

___

Something I've done recently that sparked a great learning moment was:

___

Looking ahead

One question I want to explore with my child this month is:

___

One way I can show that I'm still learning too is:

___

One message I want my child to hear from me about learning is:

___

Remember: You don't need all the answers to grow a curious child. You just need to be willing to wonder with them.

Self-reflection tool for curious teaching

Curious teachers create curious classrooms.

This reflective tool invites you to pause and consider how your beliefs, routines, and professional culture support or constrain curiosity in your practice.

My view of curiosity in learning

To me, curiosity in the classroom is ...

- ☐ A core driver of learning
- ☐ Important, but hard to prioritise
- ☐ Present in some lessons but not others
- ☐ Something I'm still figuring out how to foster

I believe curiosity is most visible when students ...

- ☐ Ask unexpected questions
- ☐ Make meaningful connections
- ☐ Challenge assumptions
- ☐ Explore ideas beyond the curriculum
- ☐ Take initiative in their learning

One thing I used to believe about curiosity that has changed:

_____

My practice as a curious teacher

When planning lessons, I regularly ...

- ☐ Build in time for open-ended inquiry
- ☐ Include space for student questions
- ☐ Use provocations or wonderings to spark interest
- ☐ Allow students to shape the learning path
- ☐ Adapt based on classroom feedback

In the last month, a time I modelled curiosity was when ...

_____

One area of my practice I'm currently exploring or experimenting with:

_____

My learning culture

In our classroom, students are encouraged to ...

- ☐ Ask 'why' and 'what if' questions
- ☐ Reflect on their learning process
- ☐ Embrace uncertainty or mistakes
- ☐ Seek multiple perspectives
- ☐ Challenge or reframe problems

In our team/staff meetings, curiosity is ...

- ☐ Encouraged and built into the routine
- ☐ Present when time allows
- ☐ Often crowded out by operational tasks
- ☐ Rare or risky

A routine or structure that enables inquiry in my classroom/team is:

_____

Barriers and possibilities

Some barriers to curiosity in my current role include:

- ☐ Time pressure and curriculum coverage
- ☐ High-stakes assessment or accountability demands
- ☐ Rigid structures or lack of flexibility
- ☐ A culture of caution or fear of 'getting it wrong'
- ☐ My own fatigue or workload

One of these barriers I feel I could begin to shift is:

_____

What support, time, or trust would make that shift possible?

_____

Looking ahead

A curious question I want to explore in my teaching this term is:

_____

Something I could try or adapt in my practice to spark more curiosity is:

_____

Someone I could talk to, observe, or learn with is:

_____

Final reflection

How is curiosity showing up in your classroom – and in you?

- ☐ It's visible, vibrant, and embedded in our learning
- ☐ It's present, but could be more deliberate
- ☐ It's there in spirit, but needs structural support
- ☐ It's been crowded out – but I'm ready to revive it

Self-reflection tool for curious principals

Leadership is about creating the conditions where curiosity can thrive.

This tool invites school leaders to reflect on how curiosity is embedded in their leadership approach, decision-making, staff development, and school culture.

My view of leadership and curiosity

To me, leading with curiosity means ...

- ☐ Asking better questions, not just finding faster answers
- ☐ Making space for staff and students to reflect and explore
- ☐ Modelling vulnerability and openness
- ☐ Holding uncertainty with care and clarity

I believe a curious school culture is most visible when ...

- ☐ Teachers talk about puzzles of practice, not just tasks
- ☐ Students ask questions that reshape the lesson
- ☐ Teams experiment and share what they learn
- ☐ Inquiry drives improvement, not compliance

One belief I hold about curiosity and leadership is:

_____

My leadership practices

In the last month, I have ...

- ☐ Asked staff for feedback on my leadership
- ☐ Protected time for team-based professional inquiry
- ☐ Started a meeting with a question rather than an update
- ☐ Shared my own learning or uncertainty with others
- ☐ Invited student voice into a decision-making process

A recent leadership moment that reflected curiosity in action was:

_____

An area of the school where curiosity could be stronger is:

_____

School culture and conditions

In our school, curiosity is ...

- ☐ A lived value, visible in staff and student practices
- ☐ Present, but not always protected
- ☐ Squeezed out by operational demands
- ☐ Starting to re-emerge through leadership or inquiry work

Our school improvement approach is driven by ...

- ☐ Compliance and performance targets
- ☐ A blend of data, dialogue, and local learning
- ☐ Shared inquiry and strategic experimentation
- ☐ A clear purpose, co-constructed with staff and students

One structure or ritual that enables curiosity at our school is:

_____

One that could be reimagined to better support inquiry is:

_____

Barriers and possibilities

Current barriers to leading with curiosity in my role include:

- ☐ Policy demands and external compliance
- ☐ Time pressure and urgent operational tasks
- ☐ Staff fatigue or change saturation
- ☐ My own leadership habits or workload
- ☐ A culture of caution or past reform overload

One of these I could begin to shift or reframe is:

_____

What would it take – for me or for my team – to make that shift possible?

_____

Looking ahead

A leadership question I want to explore this term is:

___

A conversation I could start to ignite curiosity is:

___

Someone on staff whose curiosity I want to support more is:

___

One action I will take this term to protect time or space for inquiry is:

___

Final reflection

Right now, I would describe our school's culture of curiosity as …

- ☐ Embedded and energising
- ☐ Present but needing protection
- ☐ Emerging and ready to grow
- ☐ Dormant, but ready to be rekindled

Self-reflection tool for curious system leaders

Curious systems don't deliver learning. They enable it.

This tool invites you to reflect on how your leadership fosters curiosity, not just through what you say, but through how your system works and learns.

My leadership orientation

As a system leader, I tend to lead through …

- ☐ Direction: setting priorities and delivering aligned strategies
- ☐ Enablement: creating space, time, and support for schools to learn
- ☐ Inquiry: asking questions that uncover what's working, where, and why
- ☐ Performance: ensuring accountability and measurable improvement

When I consider my leadership influence, I believe I am …

- ☐ A manager of operations
- ☐ A steward of values
- ☐ A guardian of coherence
- ☐ A catalyst for learning

The phrase that best describes my current leadership mindset is:

_____

Systems that learn

In the past 3–6 months, I have …

- ☐ Asked schools what they are noticing, not just reporting
- ☐ Made space for schools to co-design solutions or strategies
- ☐ Adapted a policy or initiative based on local insights
- ☐ Funded professional inquiry, not just training delivery
- ☐ Publicly shared my own learning or uncertainty

A recent example of systemic curiosity in action was:

_____

One area of the system where curiosity is being constrained is:

_____

Culture, coherence, and capacity

Across the system I lead, I believe ...

- ☐ Curiosity is alive in pockets, but not yet cultural
- ☐ Collaboration is structural, not just symbolic
- ☐ Professional judgment is trusted and nurtured
- ☐ Policy and accountability still crowd out reflection
- ☐ Equity is framed as access and achievement – not recognition and agency

One system ritual or process that enables curiosity is:

_____

One that could be redesigned to foster more inquiry is:

_____

Listening, learning, and letting go

As a leader, I actively ...

- ☐ Invite feedback from school leaders and frontline educators
- ☐ Shift priorities based on new insights – not just performance targets
- ☐ Protect time and space for deep learning
- ☐ Accept complexity rather than oversimplifying it
- ☐ Let go of control to enable distributed leadership

A tough but valuable moment of curiosity in my leadership recently was:

_____

A voice or perspective I need to hear more from is:

_____

System architecture

Our current system architecture is best described as ...

- ☐ Designed for delivery
- ☐ Designed for control
- ☐ Designed for inquiry
- ☐ Being redesigned to enable learning

We support collaboration and innovation through …

- ☐ Competition for funding or recognition
- ☐ Centrally approved initiatives
- ☐ Peer networks and regional learning communities
- ☐ Long-term, trust-based partnerships

Our evaluation and accountability practices …

- ☐ Focus narrowly on outcomes and data
- ☐ Balance performance and inquiry
- ☐ Include stories, reflection, and collective learning
- ☐ Need redesigning to support professional agency

Leading forward

A system-level question I want to explore further is:

_____

One policy, protocol, or routine I could rethink this year is:

_____

One thing I can stop doing to make more room for learning is:

_____

A leader I want to support more intentionally is:

_____

One way I will protect time, trust, or curiosity at scale is:

_____

Final reflection

Right now, I would describe my system's culture of curiosity as …

- ☐ Isolated and informal – reliant on individuals
- ☐ Present and emerging – supported in some areas
- ☐ Embedded and protected – part of how we lead
- ☐ In decline – crowded out by complexity or compliance

APPENDIX D
Self-Assessment Tools

The following self-assessment tools are designed to support schools, leaders, and systems to reflect on key dimensions of moral purpose, school capital, and curiosity. They are not checklists for compliance – they are mirrors for thoughtful practice and ongoing learning.

Self-assessment tool for moral purpose

Instructions: Reflect on your school's moral purpose in practice. For each statement, circle the number that best reflects your experience. Use this tool to surface shared values and identify areas to strengthen.

Response scale (circle one per item):

1. Completely describes us
2. Mostly describes us
3. Generally describes us
4. Neutral
5. Somewhat describes us
6. Barely describes us
7. Does not describe us at all

Clarity of purpose – knowing what matters

1. Our school has a clear, shared sense of why we exist and who we serve.

1	2	3	4	5	6	7

2. We regularly revisit our purpose to guide decisions and improvement efforts.

1	2	3	4	5	6	7

3. Our goals are driven by values, not just by data or external pressure.

1	2	3	4	5	6	7

4. Leaders and staff use our purpose to navigate complex or competing demands.

1	2	3	4	5	6	7

Ethical commitment – doing what's right

1. We strive to ensure every student is challenged, supported, and included.

1	2	3	4	5	6	7

2. Our staff take responsibility for the success and wellbeing of all learners.

1	2	3	4	5	6	7

3. We address inequities in opportunity and outcomes, even when it's difficult.

1	2	3	4	5	6	7

4. We act with integrity, even when no one is watching.

1	2	3	4	5	6	7

Voice and relationships – putting people at the centre

1. We listen to students, families, and staff when shaping school priorities.

1	2	3	4	5	6	7

2. Decision-making includes diverse voices, not just the loudest or most senior.

1	2	3	4	5	6	7

3. Staff and students feel seen, heard, and valued for who they are.

| 1 | 2 | 3 | 4 | 5 | 6 | 7 |

4. We build trust through relationships – not just roles or authority.

| 1 | 2 | 3 | 4 | 5 | 6 | 7 |

Alignment and action – living what we say

1. Our day-to-day practices reflect our values – not just our strategic plan.

| 1 | 2 | 3 | 4 | 5 | 6 | 7 |

2. Leaders model the behaviours they expect of others.

| 1 | 2 | 3 | 4 | 5 | 6 | 7 |

3. There is coherence between what we say, what we do, and what we reward.

| 1 | 2 | 3 | 4 | 5 | 6 | 7 |

4. We pause to ask: Does this decision reflect who we are and what we believe?

| 1 | 2 | 3 | 4 | 5 | 6 | 7 |

Scoring advice

- For each section, calculate your average score. Lower scores reflect stronger forms of capital.
- Use results to guide team discussion: Where are we strongest? Where might we stretch further?
- Don't aim for perfection – aim for awareness and action. This tool is a mirror, not a ranking.

Use these reflections to guide team conversations, uncover assumptions, and identify small actions that could build stronger moral purpose/school capital/curiosity.

Self-assessment tool for school capital

Instructions: Reflect on your school's current conditions. For each statement, circle the number that best reflects your experience. Use this tool to identify areas of strength and opportunity for growth.

Response scale (circle one per item):

1. Completely describes us
2. Mostly describes us
3. Generally describes us
4. Neutral
5. Somewhat describes us
6. Barely describes us
7. Does not describe us at all

Intellectual capital – what we know and how we share it

1. Professional learning in our school is connected to real work and real needs.

1	2	3	4	5	6	7

2. Staff regularly share practice, insights, and evidence with one another.

1	2	3	4	5	6	7

3. High-quality teaching is recognised, shared, and supported to grow further.

1	2	3	4	5	6	7

4. New knowledge is valued and used to adapt practice – not just stored in policy folders.

1	2	3	4	5	6	7

Social capital – the strength of our relationships

1. Staff trust one another to speak honestly and raise difficult issues.

1	2	3	4	5	6	7

2. There is a strong sense of collective responsibility for student learning.

1	2	3	4	5	6	7

3. Collaboration is the norm, not the exception.

1	2	3	4	5	6	7

4. We welcome diverse perspectives and value respectful disagreement.

1	2	3	4	5	6	7

Organisational capital – the way we work together

1. Our structures protect time for deep professional learning and reflection.

1	2	3	4	5	6	7

2. Meetings are focused on learning, not just logistics.

1	2	3	4	5	6	7

3. Inquiry and experimentation are encouraged and supported by leaders.

1	2	3	4	5	6	7

4. Improvement efforts are coordinated and coherent – not layered and scattered.

1	2	3	4	5	6	7

Financial capital – what we resource and why it matters

1. We invest in the tools, programs, and people that make the biggest difference.

1	2	3	4	5	6	7

2. Staff are provided with time or release to collaborate, innovate, and lead.

1	2	3	4	5	6	7

3. Resources are used transparently and aligned with our core values.

1	2	3	4	5	6	7

4. We find ways to support curiosity, equity, and innovation – even with limited funding.

1	2	3	4	5	6	7

Scoring advice

- For each section, calculate your average score. Lower scores reflect stronger forms of capital.
- Use results to guide team discussion: Where are we strongest? Where might we stretch further?
- Don't aim for perfection – aim for awareness and action. This tool is a mirror, not a ranking.

Use these reflections to guide team conversations, uncover assumptions, and identify small actions that could build stronger moral purpose/school capital/curiosity.

Self-assessment tool for curiosity

Instructions: Reflect on your own leadership practice. For each statement, circle the number that best reflects your current experience. Use this tool to notice patterns, strengths, and opportunities to deepen curiosity in your leadership.

Response scale (circle one per item):

1. Completely describes me
2. Mostly describes me
3. Generally describes me
4. Neutral
5. Somewhat describes me
6. Barely describes me
7. Does not describe me at all

Finding energy and motivation in new questions and ideas

1. I feel energised by uncovering fresh ideas and future possibilities.

1	2	3	4	5	6	7

2. I stay curious about what's possible in our school – even under pressure.

1	2	3	4	5	6	7

3. I actively explore new leadership ideas, research, and perspectives.

1	2	3	4	5	6	7

4. I model inquisitiveness and intellectual humility in how I lead.

1	2	3	4	5	6	7

Digging into challenges to uncover deeper understanding

1. I feel compelled to explore the root causes of persistent school issues.

1	2	3	4	5	6	7

2. I seek patterns and insights – not just quick solutions – when problems arise.

1	2	3	4	5	6	7

3. I use data, feedback, and dialogue to understand what's really happening.

1	2	3	4	5	6	7

4. I revisit problems until I feel confident we've explored them fully.

1	2	3	4	5	6	7

Staying open and responsive when stakes are high

1. I stay curious, even in difficult conversations or moments of conflict.

1	2	3	4	5	6	7

2. I'm willing to try new leadership strategies, even when outcomes are uncertain.

1	2	3	4	5	6	7

3. I manage the tension between decisiveness and inquiry.

1	2	3	4	5	6	7

4. I use setbacks as learning opportunities, not just performance gaps.

1	2	3	4	5	6	7

Welcoming insight from across and beyond the school

1. I listen deeply to students, staff, families, and peers.

   | 1 | 2 | 3 | 4 | 5 | 6 | 7 |

2. I seek feedback from those with different perspectives – even when it's hard to hear.

   | 1 | 2 | 3 | 4 | 5 | 6 | 7 |

3. I regularly ask: 'What am I missing?' or 'Whose voice is not in the room?'

   | 1 | 2 | 3 | 4 | 5 | 6 | 7 |

4. I treat my work as an evolving craft, not a fixed identity.

   | 1 | 2 | 3 | 4 | 5 | 6 | 7 |

Scoring advice

For each section, calculate your average score. Lower scores indicate stronger orientation toward that dimension of leadership curiosity.

Use your responses to reflect: Where does my curiosity thrive? Where could it stretch further? How does my curiosity influence the school culture?

Use these reflections to guide team conversations, uncover assumptions, and identify small actions that could build stronger moral purpose/school capital/curiosity.

APPENDIX E
Literary and Cultural Touchstones

The quotes that open each chapter were chosen to evoke the spirit of inquiry, resilience, purpose, and curiosity that animates this book. They remind us that wisdom often travels through story, art, and metaphor – not only through data and policy.

Prologue

'We're all mad here.' – The Cheshire Cat, *Alice's Adventures in Wonderland*

The Cat reminds us that in unfamiliar territory – like the pursuit of lasting school improvement – a little madness is simply part of the landscape. To ask bold questions and embrace uncertainty is not folly; it is wisdom in disguise.

Chapter 1

'Curiouser and curiouser!' – Lewis Carroll

This quote appears in *Alice's Adventures in Wonderland* (1865) when Alice exclaims in astonishment as the surreal world around her becomes increasingly strange. It has since become a cultural shorthand for wonder and bewilderment.

Chapter 2

'You don't need a weatherman to know which way the wind blows.' – Bob Dylan

From Dylan's 1965 song 'Subterranean Homesick Blues', this lyric critiques conformity and blind allegiance to authority. The phrase later inspired the name of the radical Weather Underground movement in the U.S.

Chapter 3

'We each have a responsibility to make the world a better place – bit by bit, small gesture by small gesture.' – Nick Cave

This quote is from a 2020 post on Nick Cave's *The Red Hand Files*, an online platform where he responds to fans' letters with reflections on art, faith, grief, and morality. This quote captures his emphasis on personal, everyday ethics.

Chapter 4

'You just have to look, it's always been here.' – Charles Jenkins

This lyric comes from Melbourne singer-songwriter Charles Jenkins' song 'Everything You Need Is Right Here' (2009), a warm, grounded reminder of sufficiency and presence, often associated with a sense of community and rootedness.

Chapter 5

'Tell me, what is it you plan to do with your one wild and precious life?' – Mary Oliver

From the poem 'The Summer Day' (1992) by Pulitzer Prize-winning poet Mary Oliver, this line is a widely quoted prompt to reflect on purpose, mortality, and the beauty of the present moment.

Interlude

'Two roads diverged in a yellow wood ...' – Robert Frost

The opening line of 'The Road Not Taken' (1916), one of Robert Frost's most famous poems. It explores themes of choice, individuality, and the human tendency to assign meaning to decisions in hindsight.

Chapter 6

'What the roots drink, the leaves whisper.' – Rumi

A paraphrase or poetic rendering attributed to Jalāl al-Dīn Rūmī, the 13th-century Persian poet and Sufi mystic. While not a direct translation, it captures Rumi's recurring theme of hidden influence and interconnectedness in spiritual growth.

Chapter 7

'Justice is what love looks like in public.' – Cornel West

Cornel West, American philosopher and activist, has used this phrase in public speeches and writings to define justice as an active, embodied form of love applied to social and political life – often in the context of racial and economic equity.

Chapter 8

'Be patient toward all that is unsolved in your heart and try to love the questions themselves.' – Rainer Maria Rilke

From *Letters to a Young Poet* (1929), Rilke's correspondence with a young writer. This quote encourages embracing uncertainty and the slow unfolding of understanding – especially relevant in reflective or creative work.

Chapter 9

'Systems resist change – but not forever.' – Margaret Wheatley

This line reflects the work of leadership thinker Margaret J. Wheatley, particularly in her books *Leadership and the New Science* (1992) and *Who Do We Choose To Be?* (2017), in which she explores complexity, systems, and change in organisations.

Chapter 10

'There is a crack in everything, that's how the light gets in.' – Leonard Cohen

From Cohen's 1992 song 'Anthem', this lyric is a poetic meditation on imperfection, resilience, and redemption. It has become an emblem of hope and flawed beauty.

Epilogue

'Hope is not the conviction that something will turn out well, but the certainty that something is worth doing, no matter how it turns out.' – Václav Havel

From Havel's essay 'Disturbing the Peace' (1986), published in the collection *Living in Truth*. Havel was a Czech playwright, essayist, dissident, and later president of Czechoslovakia (and then the Czech Republic), whose leadership emerged from his moral and intellectual resistance to totalitarianism.

References

Alexander, R. (2008). *Towards dialogic teaching: Rethinking classroom talk* (4th ed.). Dialogos.
Ashenden, D. (2024). *Unbeaching the whale: Can Australia's schooling be reformed?* Inside Story Publishing.
Ball, S. J. (2003). The teacher's soul and the terrors of performativity. *Journal of Education Policy, 18*(2), 215-28.
Bandura, A. (1997). *Self-efficacy: The exercise of control*. W. H. Freeman.
Berger, R. (2003). *An ethic of excellence: Building a culture of craftsmanship with students*. Heinemann.
Berliner, D. C. (2006). Our impoverished view of educational reform. *Teachers College Record, 108*(6), 949-95.
Biesta, G. (2020). *Educational research: An unorthodox introduction*. Bloomsbury Publishing.
Black Dog Institute. (2023). *National Teacher Survey - Summary (Preliminary Data)*. https://www.blackdoginstitute.org.au/wp-content/uploads/2021/08/National-Teacher-Survey_Summary_FEB_2023_final.pdf
Bransford, J. D., Brown, A. L., & Cocking, R. R. (Eds.). (2000). *How people learn: Brain, mind, experience, and school*. National Academy Press.
Breakspear, S., & Ryrie Jones, B. (2021). *Teaching sprints: How overloaded educators can keep getting better*. Corwin Press.
Brown, B. (2018). *Dare to lead: Brave work. Tough conversations. Whole hearts.* Random House.
Bryk, A. S., & Schneider, B. (2002). *Trust in schools: A core resource for improvement*. Russell Sage Foundation.
Bryk, A. S., Gomez, L. M., Grunow, A., & LeMahieu, P. G. (2015). *Learning to improve: How America's schools can get better at getting better*. Harvard Education Press.
Bryk, A. S., Sebring, P. B., Allensworth, E., Luppescu, S., & Easton, J. Q. (2010). *Organizing schools for improvement: Lessons from Chicago*. University of Chicago Press.
Caldwell, B. J., & Harris, J. (2008). *Why not the best schools?* ACER Press.
Campbell, E. (2003). *The ethical teacher*. Open University Press.
Claxton, G. (2008). *What's the point of school? Rediscovering the heart of education*. Oneworld Publications.
Coburn, C. E. (2003). Rethinking scale: Moving beyond numbers to deep and lasting change. *Educational Researcher, 32*(6), 3-12.
Cochran-Smith, M., & Lytle, S. L. (2009). *Inquiry as stance: Practitioner research for the next generation*. Teachers College Press.
Coleman, J. S., et al. (1966). *Equality of educational opportunity*. U.S. Government Printing Office.
Connell, R. (2013). The neoliberal cascade and education: An essay on the market agenda and its consequences. *Critical Studies in Education, 54*(2), 99-112.
Craig, W. (2025). *The curious cat and the quest for school improvement: Unpacking the impact on student learning of school SES, workplace curiosity, moral purpose, and school capital*. PhD thesis, University of Melbourne.
Cuban, L. (1990). Reforming again, again, and again. *Educational Researcher, 19*(1), 3-13.
Darling-Hammond, L. (2010). *The flat world and education: How America's commitment to equity will determine our future*. Teachers College Press.
Delpit, L. (2006). *Other people's children: Cultural conflict in the classroom*. The New Press.
Dewey, J. (1938). *Experience and education*. Macmillan.

Donohoo, J., Hattie, J., & Eells, R. (2016). The power of collective efficacy. *Educational Leadership, 73*(6), 40–44.

Durant, W. (1926). *The story of philosophy: The lives and opinions of the world's greatest philosophers.* Simon and Schuster.

D'Warte, J., & Slaughter, Y. (2023). Examining plurilingual repertoires: A focus on policy, practice, and assessment in the Australian context. In S. Melo-Pfeifer & C. Ollivier (Eds.), *Assessment of plurilingual competence and plurilingual learners in educational settings: Educative issues and empirical approaches* (pp. 62–75). Routledge.

Eacott, S. (2017). School leadership and the cult of the guru: The neo-Taylorism of Hattie. *School Leadership & Management, 37*(4), 413–26.

Edmondson, A. C. (1999). Psychological safety and learning behavior in work teams. *Administrative Science Quarterly, 44*(2), 350–83.

Edmondson, A. C. (2019). *The fearless organization: Creating psychological safety in the workplace for learning, innovation, and growth.* Wiley.

Engel, S. (2011). Children's need to know: Curiosity in schools. *Harvard Educational Review, 81*(4), 625–45.

Engel, S. (2015). *The hungry mind: The origins of curiosity in childhood.* Harvard University Press.

Fischetti, J., & Keddie, A. (2021). Leadership for inclusive education. In P. Earley & T. Greany (Eds.), *School leadership and education system reform* (pp. 105–18). Bloomsbury.

Fullan, M. (2003). *The moral imperative of school leadership.* Corwin Press.

Fullan, M. (2006). The future of educational change: System thinkers in action. *Journal of Educational Change, 7*(3), 113–22.

Fullan, M. (2011). *Choosing the wrong drivers for whole system reform.* Centre for Strategic Education.

Fullan, M. (2015). *Freedom to change: Four strategies to put your inner drive into overdrive.* Jossey-Bass.

Fullan, M., & Gallagher, M. J. (2020). *The devil is in the details: System solutions for equity, excellence, and well-being.* Corwin Press.

Fullan, M., & Hargreaves, A. (2016). *Bringing the profession back in: Call to action.* Centre for Strategic Education.

Fullan, M., & Quinn, J. (2016). *Coherence: The right drivers in action for schools, districts, and systems.* Corwin Press.

Gale, T., & Parker, S. (2017). Retaining students in Australian higher education: Cultural capital, field distinction. *European Educational Research Journal, 16*(4), 460–79.

Gallup. (2014). *State of America's schools: The path to winning again in education.* Gallup, Inc. https://www.gallup.com/education/269648/state-america-schools-report.aspx

Gardner, H., Csikszentmihalyi, M., & Damon, W. (2001). *Good work: When excellence and ethics meet.* Basic Books.

Gobby, B. (2013). Enacting the Independent Public Schools program in Western Australia. *Australian Educational Researcher, 40*(4), 511–26.

Gobby, B., & Mockler, N. (2022). *Globalising educational accountabilities.* Routledge.

Gonski, D., et al. (2018). *Through growth to achievement: Report of the review to achieve educational excellence in Australian schools.* Commonwealth of Australia.

Gruber, M. J., Gelman, B. D., & Ranganath, C. (2014). States of curiosity modulate hippocampus-dependent learning via the dopaminergic circuit. *Neuron, 84*(2), 486–96.

Halbert, J., & Kaser, L. (2013). *Spirals of inquiry: For equity and quality.* B.C. Principals' and Vice-Principals' Association.

Hannon, V., & Mackay, A. (2023). *A new politics for transforming education: Towards an effective way forward* (Leading Education Series No. 14). Centre for Strategic Education.

Hardy, I. (2015). Data, documents and discourse: Progressing the educational reforms of the Australian government. *Journal of Education Policy, 30*(4), 443–56.

Hargreaves, A., & Ainscow, M. (2015). The top and bottom of leadership and change. *Phi Delta Kappan, 97*(3), 42–48.

Hargreaves, A., & Fullan, M. (2012). *Professional capital: Transforming teaching in every school.* Teachers College Press.

Hargreaves, A., & Shirley, D. (2009). *The fourth way: The inspiring future for educational change.* Corwin Press.

Hargreaves, D. H. (2001). A capital theory of school effectiveness and improvement. *British Educational Research Journal, 27*(4), 487–503.

Harris, A. (2010). Leading system-wide improvement. In P. Peterson, E. Baker, & B. McGaw (Eds.), *International encyclopedia of education* (3rd ed., pp. 378-83). Elsevier.

Harris, A., & Jones, M. (2015). Transforming education systems: Comparative and critical perspectives on school leadership. *Asia Pacific Journal of Education, 35*(3), 311-18.

Hatano, G., & Inagaki, K. (1986). Two courses of expertise. In H. Stevenson, H. Azuma, & K. Hakuta (Eds.), *Child development and education in Japan* (pp. 262-72). W. H. Freeman.

Hattie, J. (2008). *Visible learning: A synthesis of over 800 meta-analyses relating to achievement.* Routledge.

hooks, b. (1994). *Teaching to transgress: Education as the practice of freedom.* Routledge.

Hopkins, D. (2007). *Every school a great school: Realizing the potential of system leadership.* Open University Press.

Hopkins, D. (2020). Exploding the implementation plateau: What next in school improvement? In *Exploding the implementation plateau* (pp. 9-19). Australian Council for Educational Leaders.

Hopkins, D. (2024). *Unleashing greatness: A strategy for school improvement.* Teacher Solutions.

Hopkins, D., & Craig, W. (2016). *Curiosity and powerful learning.* McREL International.

Jensen, B. (2013). *The five critical ingredients of effective teaching and learning.* Grattan Institute.

Kahneman, D. (2011). *Thinking, fast and slow.* Farrar, Straus and Giroux.

Kashdan, T. B. (2009). *Curious? Discover the missing ingredient to a fulfilling life.* HarperCollins.

Kashdan, T. B., Rose, P., & Fincham, F. D. (2004). Curiosity and exploration: Facilitating positive subjective experiences and personal growth opportunities. *Journal of Personality Assessment, 82*(3), 291-305.

Kashdan, T. B., & Silvia, P. J. (2009). Curiosity and interest: The benefits of thriving on novelty and challenge. In S. J. Lopez & C. R. Snyder (Eds.), *The Oxford handbook of positive psychology* (2nd ed., pp. 367-74). Oxford University Press.

Kashdan, T. B., Disabato, D. J., Goodman, F. R., McKnight, P. E., & Kashdan, C. (2020). The five-dimensional curiosity scale: Capturing the bandwidth of curiosity and identifying four unique subgroups of curious people. *Journal of Research in Personality, 89*, 104-117.

Ladson-Billings, G. (1995). Toward a theory of culturally relevant pedagogy. *American Educational Research Journal, 32*(3), 465-91.

Ladwig, J., & Luke, A. (2014). Does improving school mean transforming teaching? *Teacher Development, 18*(2), 161-77.

Lamb, S., Glover, S., & Walstab, A. (2014). *Educational disadvantage and regional and rural schools.* Centre for Research on Education Systems, University of Melbourne.

Lamb, S., Maire, Q., & Doecke, E. (2020). *Equity in Australian education: Measurement and meaning.* Centre for International Research on Education Systems, Victoria University.

Lampert, J. (2022). Ensuring Indigenous knowledges and perspectives inform school practices. In N. Taylor, S. Riddle, & R. Macmillan (Eds.), *Educational leadership as a culturally constructed practice* (pp. 123-40). Springer.

Leithwood, K., & Riehl, C. (2005). What we know about successful school leadership. In W. A. Firestone & C. Riehl (Eds.), *A new agenda for research in educational leadership* (pp. 22-47). Teachers College Press.

Lieberman, A., & Miller, L. (2004). *Teacher leadership.* Jossey-Bass.

Lingard, B. (2010). Policy borrowing, policy learning: Testing times in Australian schooling. *Critical Studies in Education, 51*(2), 129-47.

Lingard, B., & McGregor, G. (2014). Two contrasting Australian curriculum responses to globalisation: What students should learn or become. *The Curriculum Journal, 25*(1), 90-110.

Lingard, B., Sellar, S., & Savage, G. (2014). Rearticulating social justice as equity in schooling policy: The effects of testing and data infrastructures. *British Journal of Sociology of Education, 35*(5), 710-30.

Lingard, B., Thompson, G., & Sellar, S. (2016). *National testing, school reform and student achievement: An Australian story.* Routledge.

Loewenstein, G. (1994). The psychology of curiosity: A review and reinterpretation. *Psychological Bulletin, 116*(1), 75-98.

Mehta, J., & Fine, S. (2019). *In search of deeper learning: The quest to remake the American high school.* Harvard University Press.

Mitchell, C., & Sackney, L. (2011). *Profound improvement: Building capacity for a learning community.* Routledge.

Mockler, N. (2011). Beyond 'what works': Understanding teacher identity as a practical and political tool. *Teachers and Teaching: Theory and Practice, 17*(5), 517–28.

OECD. (2019a). *OECD teaching and learning international survey (TALIS) 2018 results: Teachers and school leaders as lifelong learners.* OECD Publishing.

OECD. (2019b). *PISA 2018 results (Volume I): What students know and can do.* OECD Publishing.

Palmer, P. J. (1998). *The courage to teach: Exploring the inner landscape of a teacher's life.* Jossey-Bass.

Priestley, M., & Biesta, G. J. J. (2013). *Reinventing the curriculum: New trends in curriculum policy and practice.* Bloomsbury.

Priestley, M., Biesta, G. J. J., & Robinson, S. (2015). *Teacher agency: An ecological approach.* Bloomsbury.

Reid, A. (2019). *Changing Australian education: How policy is taking us backwards and what can be done about it.* Allen & Unwin.

Ritchhart, R., Church, M., & Morrison, K. (2011). *Making thinking visible: How to promote engagement, understanding, and independence for all learners.* Jossey-Bass.

Robinson, V. M. J., Hohepa, M., & Lloyd, C. (2009). *School leadership and student outcomes: Identifying what works and why: Best evidence synthesis iteration (BES).* Ministry of Education, New Zealand.

Rumsfeld, D. (2002, February 12). *DoD news briefing – Secretary Rumsfeld and Gen. Myers.* U.S. Department of Defense. https://www.defense.gov/News/Transcripts/Transcript/Article/1692009/

Sahlberg, P. (2011). *Finnish lessons: What can the world learn from educational change in Finland?* Teachers College Press.

Sahlberg, P. (2016). Global education reform movement and its impact on schooling. In D. Hung & K. M. Lee (Eds.), *Educational innovations beyond technology: Nurturing leadership and establishing learning organizations* (pp. 128–43). Springer.

Santoro, D. A. (2018). *Demoralized: Why teachers leave the profession they love and how they can stay.* Harvard Education Press.

Senge, P. M. (1990). *The fifth discipline: The art and practice of the learning organization.* Doubleday.

Sharratt, L., & Fullan, M. (2009). *Realization: The change imperative for deepening district-wide reform.* Corwin Press.

Sharratt, L., & Fullan, M. (2012). *Putting faces on the data: What great leaders do!* Corwin Press.

Smyth, J. (2011). *The socially just school: Making space for youth to speak back.* Peter Lang.

Spillane, J. P. (2006). *Distributed leadership.* Jossey-Bass.

Stoll, L., & Louis, K. S. (2007). *Professional learning communities: Divergence, depth and dilemmas.* Open University Press.

Stoll, L., Bolam, R., McMahon, A., Wallace, M., & Thomas, S. (2006). Professional learning communities: A review of the literature. *Journal of Educational Change, 7*(4), 221–58.

TEMAG [Teacher Education Ministerial Advisory Group]. (2015). *Action now: Classroom ready teachers.* Australian Government Department of Education and Training.

Thomson, S., De Bortoli, L., & Underwood, C. (2020). *PISA 2018: Reporting Australia's results. Volume II: Student and school characteristics.* ACER.

Timperley, H. (2011). *Realizing the power of professional learning.* Open University Press.

Timperley, H., Kaser, L., & Halbert, J. (2007). *Teacher professional learning and development.* International Academy of Education & International Bureau of Education.

Timperley, H., Kaser, L., & Halbert, J. (2014). *A framework for transforming learning in schools: Innovation and the spiral of inquiry.* Centre for Strategic Education.

Timperley, H., Wilson, A., Barrar, H., & Fung, I. (2007). *Teacher professional learning and development: Best evidence synthesis iteration (BES).* New Zealand Ministry of Education.

Tyack, D., & Tobin, W. (1994). The 'grammar' of schooling: Why has it been so hard to change? *American Educational Research Journal, 31*(3), 453–79.

Wheatley, M. J. (2002). *Turning to one another: Simple conversations to restore hope to the future.* Berrett-Koehler.

www.ingramcontent.com/pod-product-compliance
Lightning Source LLC
Chambersburg PA
CBHW052022070526
44584CB00016B/1865